w

Other Highland Books
  by Paul Tournier
    *The Adventure of Living*
    *Escape from Loneliness*
    *A Doctor's Casebook in the Light of the Bible*
    *Marriage Difficulties*
    *Secrets*
    *A Place for You*
  by Michael Green
    *Evangelism in the Early Church*
  by Edith Schaeffer
    *What Is a Family?*
  by John L. Sherrill
    *They Speak with Other Tongues*
  edited by Edward England
    *A Way With Words*

# A LONDON SPARROW

**Phyllis Thompson**

HIGHLAND BOOKS

ISBN 0 946616 10 8

Printed in Great Britain for Highland Books, a division
of Edward England Books, Crowton House, The Broad-
way, Crowborough, E. Sussex TN6 1AB, by Richard
Clay (The Chaucer Press) Ltd, Bungay, Suffolk.

# *Foreword*

This book will give pleasure and encouragement all over the world. The author has herself what she claims for her subject – "the skill of the true story-teller" – and makes you feel it all happening as you read.

One high value is that before the close of Chapter 8 we are in the *sequel* to the story that is so well known and taken beyond the Edinburgh House B.B.C. "Undefeated" booklet, Alan Burgess's classic "The Small Woman" and that very popular film, "The Inn of the Sixth Happiness". Now we have the full picture. Now we know what happened in the last thirty years of Gladys Aylward's adventurous life, including the "This is Your Life" television episode.

The *beginnings* are also filled in for us. How good to know that following her upbringing in a Christian home, it all really came to life when the Rev. F. W. Pitt (known years ago to great monthly audiences at Kingsway Hall) and his wife were used of God in her conversion. There are other details, too, that are in neither of the two books nor the film, filling out the portrait and telling the whole epic tale.

You will be disturbed at some of the things you read in this book. Her Chinese attitude to things, for one. You will be challenged. Her utterly selfless compassion for others, for example, and you will be intrigued. Her premonition over the rape of Tibet, her simple creed, insight into her romance and how God compensated her – all are here for you. You will revel in tributes paid to her by Dr. Hoyte of the Borden Memorial Hospital on the banks of the Yellow River, by the public schoolboy ("It was the way she talked about God, as though she knew Him"), and by the celebrated Chinese author, Hsu Soo.

But read it for yourself, the life story of Ai Weh Teh, "The Virtuous One", and gird up your loins! As she herself translated a verse in 1 Chronicles 22 from her Chinese Bible: *"Do not be afraid and do not wobble. Is not your God with you?"*

GEOFFREY R. KING

# Acknowledgements

To obtain accurate information about Gladys Aylward, of whom so much has been written and reported, has been a task full of surprises. Some of the things I expected to find I could not – other things that I had not looked for emerged! My personal acquaintance with her commenced in China, in the early 1940's, but I met her only infrequently after that, and I am deeply indebted to many people who knew her personally, some of whom were even able to produce letters she had written to them – very welcome grist for the biographer's mill! Many have provided information based on personal knowledge of her, and when it comes to acknowledging them all it is easier to know where to begin than where to end. Those who were her relatives, friends, colleagues and acquaintances have, in almost every case, willingly shared with me their reminiscences of her when asked to do so. The amassed evidence of many people has been invaluable to me in presenting, to the best of my ability, an accurate picture of her life and character. If at any point, through lack of information, I have conveyed a wrong impression, I am sorry.

Her life falls naturally into four periods of time, when she made her home in different countries. I would like to thank all those whose names are listed below, at the stages in which they came into her life, for the help they have given me.

1902–32 ENGLAND. Mrs. Violet Braithwaite, Mr. L. Aylward, Mrs. Queenie Cocup, Mr. and Mrs. J. Jago, Miss Ada Warin, Mrs. L. Gaussen.

1932–49 CHINA. The Rev. and Mrs. David Davies, Dr. Stanley Hoyte, Mr. and Mrs. H. Fisher, Dr. Handley Stockley, Miss Annie Skau, Mr. and Mrs. S. Jeffery, Mr. and Mrs. D. Woodward, Dr. Olin Stockwell, Major Jarvis Tien, Mrs. R. Butler, Mr. Julius Bergstrom, Dr. Francis Chu, Mr. and Mrs. A. Saunders, Mrs. N. Douty, Miss J. Woodward, Mrs. D. McCammon, Miss Grace Jephson, Mr. N. Blake, Mr. and Mrs. G. Vinden.

1949–57 ENGLAND. Miss Ruby Rook, Miss Violet Bralant, Mrs. R. Tyndale-Biscoe, Mrs. H. Gordon-Dean, the Rev. S. Wang, Miss Esme Wilson, Sister D. Gemmell, Mr. L. T. Lyall, the Rev. Geoffrey R. King, the Rev. the Hon. Roland Lamb, the Rev. F. Harding, Mr. and Mrs. P. Parry, Mr. Alan Burgess, Miss Nada Cholerton, Mr. J. Erskine Tuck.

1957–70 TAIWAN. Dr. D. Dale, Mrs. Esther Huang, Mr. Reuben Wang, the Rev. Clifford Liu, Mr. Leslie Huang, Miss K.

## ACKNOWLEDGEMENTS

Langton-Smith, Mrs. E. W. Carlburg, Mrs. Lilian Dickson, Mrs. Twinem, Mrs. Lilian Martin, Miss M. Sells, the Rev. Samuel Wu, Dr. Abraham Mok, Mr. Chester Cheong, the Rev. Bernard Barron, Mr. E. E. Cooke.

I am especially grateful to Mrs. Roland Lamb for lending me Miss Aylward's Chinese Bible, her school report, and personal letters written to a friend during her early years in China; to the Advent Testimony and Preparation Movement for permission to quote from the leaflet "An Air Raid in China"; to Mr. Yang of the Christian Witness Press for obtaining permission to quote from an article in the Chinese magazine, *Good Tidings Monthly*; to Mrs. Gladys Donnithorne, Mrs. I. Teasdale and the Rev. J. McNicol for exceptional help given in collecting material; to the Overseas Missionary Fellowship for help and hospitality generously given in Hong Kong and Taiwan, and also for providing extracts from their Candidates Committee Minutes; to Chaplain Malliett of the U.S. Navy for a tape recording of an address given by Miss Aylward; to Mr. Alan Burgess and the Rev. Bernard Barron for sharing their reminiscences so willingly; and to Mrs. Violet Braithwaite, for intimate and colourful glimpses into the Aylward home life, and her encouragement in the writing of her sister's biography.

Three people read the MS through critically – Miss Violet Bralant from the point of view of a personal friend, Mr. Arthur Saunders as one with many years' experience in China and among the Chinese, and Mr. E. E. Cooke as a Trustee of the Gladys Aylward Trust from 1966, and as one of her Executors. I am extremely grateful to them for their conscientious scrutiny, and have been glad to act on their corrections and suggestions.

Lastly, I thank the publishers for entrusting me with the task of writing this biography of an ordinary little woman who became famous in a materialistic age because, as far as she was concerned, God was not dead, but very much alive.

PHYLLIS THOMPSON
London, 1971

# Contents

# CHAPTER ONE

# *The Parlourmaid*

The telephone was ringing insistently, like an alarm clock, and the diminutive housemaid in her neat uniform and crisp white apron eyed it rather uneasily. A heavy aggressive-looking thing it was, standing there with the receiver hanging on a hook, trembling slightly now from the vibration of that continuous raucous clangour. She knew there was no-one else in the house but herself to lift the receiver, so she advanced determinedly towards it, held it to her ear, and shouted down the protruding nozzle,

"Hullo."

A faint female voice at the other end of the line asked to speak to her mistress.

"She's out," said Gladys shortly.

"Oh. Well, will you tell her that I shan't be able to come and see her after all," said the voice, adding in explanation, "I've got scarlet fever."

That was the end of the conversation, for Gladys slammed the receiver back on its hook and retreated rapidly. As she explained when relating the incident later,

"I didn't want her germs!"

There were plenty of family jokes in the Aylward home in Edmonton, and this was typical of them. It was just like "our Glad" to see an army of germs travelling at the same speed as sound along the telegraph wires and then leaping at her through the mouthpiece of the telephone! Dad and Mum had long since recognised that their eldest child was not what might be called the brainy type. That report card covering her last four years at school had been revealing. Conduct and personal neatness were excellent from first to last, she "attacked her difficulties vigorously," and was very much in earnest about her work. When it came to native talent however, her position in class told its own story. The nearest she ever got to the top was seventh and the farthest from it fifty-third, and that could not all be accounted for by absences due to bad health. Composition was good though writing poor, and there was an ever recurring reference to the weakness of her arithmetic.

What she lacked in intellectual attainments she made up for in doggedness and high spirits, and when she came home on her day off the place hummed, for Mum had plenty to say, too. They'd talk and they'd laugh, and they'd mimic the people they'd met, Violet joining in, and then one of them would get irritable, and there would be a snappy retort, and laughter would turn to angry tears, and the sparks would fly until they all subsided in sulky silence, and Dad, who was used to these scenes, would say quietly from his corner,

"Well, have you finished now?" and they'd smile sheepishly and everything would be all right again.

"All we Whiskins are a bit mad," Mum used to say sometimes. She was a Whiskin before she married Dad, a thorough-going little Cockney with her ready wit and her love for bright colours and plenty of feathers in her hat, when hats had feathers in them. It was no wonder she had caught Dad's eye in the Post Office where she worked and where, being a postman, he had to go and collect the registered letters. It was another of the family jokes, the way he'd been too shy to speak to her, so slipped a letter across the counter to her instead, asking if he could take her out for a walk. Two or three letters were slipped back and forth across the counter before she agreed to meet him, and then when she turned up, dressed as smart as you like, he wasn't there – he was walking up and down on the pavement on the other side of the road, unable to pluck up the courage to cross over and speak to her! Well, he'd had to face the music next morning! Mum had fairly hissed at him, like an angry little cat with all its fur on end, demanding that he should give an account of his ungentlemanly behaviour, and then going on to tell him, in fluent and colourful language, the utter contempt with which she regarded him, until the sight of his woebegone face suddenly made her stop. They looked across the counter at each other in silence, then she giggled and he laughed, and in the inexplicable way these things happen, the whole course of their lives was settled in that moment.

Everything was conducted in the accepted manner, of course. They started walking out, then became engaged, she cramming things into her bottom drawer while he saved for all he was worth, until on April 8th, 1900, they were married, and after a year or so in Bermondsey went to live in Edmonton, in the north of London.

It was here, on 24th February, 1902, that their first child was born. She was christened Gladys May, and when she was old enough they took her to church with them, sent her to Sunday School, and when she was four-teen found a job for her as assistant in the Penny Bazaar.

9

This was a highly exciting place, which had nothing on sale that cost more than a penny, but which nevertheless was able to display a great variety of articles, suitable for all sorts of uses, and Gladys announced triumphantly that she now saw how she could buy all her Christmas presents for sixpence. After a time she left the Penny Bazaar and went to serve in a grocer's shop. But then the men started returning from the First World War, wanting their jobs back, so although it meant leaving home Gladys had to go into service.

She did not stay anywhere for long. "Can't settle down," said Dad. "Never know when she'll be on the doorstep, come home again till she gets another job!" Eventually she found herself as a parlourmaid in the West End of London.

Domestic servants had a hard time of it in those days after the First World War, with long hours and small pay. But as far as Gladys was concerned she enjoyed life, especially in London where there were compensations which balanced the disadvantages. Wasn't she in the heart of the great city, with its lights and its theatres, its glimpses of gentlemen in long tails escorting bejewelled ladies in gleaming silks and satins, its gay sounds of music from the orchestras in the hotels and restaurants? There was the darker side of life, too, to stir the imagination with its pathos and its passion – little ragged children, tramps on the embankment sleeping under sheets of newspapers as the trams went clanging by, women with scarlet lips and faces heavy with powder standing at street corners when twilight descended. And there were the ordinary people thronging the streets, the good-natured, grumbling Londoners whom she knew and understood so well. She loved it all, the policemen on beat, the red pillar boxes, the newsvendors, the mothers pushing prams and the buses rumbling by.

And she liked being so near to the theatres. You could get in for a few pence if you queued up for the cheap seats. "I'll take you to Drury Lane on Saturday," she would say to Queenie. Queenie was her cousin, and lived in Fulham, not far from where she was working, and as the little schoolgirl's mother had died Gladys felt sorry for her, and often took her out. Breathlessly, heads pushed forward, they followed the anguished but musical adventures of beautiful, innocent blondes whose torments usually had a happy ending as they minced shyly towards the strong, silent men whose hearts had been nearly broken (but not quite) by all that had gone before.

"Wish I could be an actress," breathed Gladys, blinking as the glaring electric lights brought her back to stark reality from the dim world of romance. Rosy dreams of holding audiences spell-bound with the limelight playing on her had to be suspended, however, for she must get indoors before the mistress started hovering round in the hall, ready to enquire suspiciously why she was late. Back in the twenties the fear that girls might "get into trouble" haunted the minds of those responsible for them, and young housemaids were expected to be in not a minute after ten when they had an evening off.

Once safely indoors the dreams would return, and if Gladys did not have much opportunity to indulge in the smoking, dancing, gambling and nights out at the theatre to which she sometimes referred in later years, it was not for lack of thinking about these delights. For the most part they had to be enjoyed in imagination, not in fact, and she was going nowhere in particular one Tuesday evening when a group of young people standing outside a church spotted her, smilingly invited her to come inside, then linked arms through hers and led her half-laughing, half-protesting, into the building.

She was rather annoyed. She sat through the service inwardly resentful, yet unwillingly compelled by the preacher's eloquence to pay attention to what he said. There was nothing in it that she had not heard before. All that about God being alive, and knowing what was going on in people's hearts as well as in their lives, and there being a time when everybody would have to stand before Him and give account of themselves. Of course she had heard things like that before, and about God loving people and being willing to forgive them when they'd done wrong, too. She'd heard about God from the time she could remember, but never before with this alarming sense of reality. She was hurrying to get away when it was all over when someone at the door grasped her hand, enquired her name, and then said,

"Miss Aylward, I believe God is wanting you."

Gladys was alarmed.

"No fear!" she said quickly. "I don't want any of that!" and scurried off, out of reach of that firm hand, but not out of earshot of the voice that called out something to the effect that she might not want God, but God wanted her.

It was a disturbing experience because, unlike the exciting impressions left by a visit to the theatre, it made her feel uneasy, as though she had done something wrong but she didn't know what it was. And instead of fading away, this sense of uneasiness increased until she was thoroughly miserable.

Eventually she decided to go and see the clergyman in charge of the church where the meeting had been held. The Rev. F. W. Pitt was his name and when she got to his house and rang the bell, it was to be told that he was out. Would she like to come in and have a talk with her instead the clergyman's wife asked? So in Gladys went and told her all about it.

The clergyman's wife was sympathetic, but not particularly surprised. She seemed to understand what was going on inside Gladys better than Gladys did herself. The gist of what she told her was that she was out of touch with God. It was God she needed, and it was Jesus Christ who could put her in touch with Him.

There was really nothing new in this, either. Gladys had heard it time and time again.

> He died that we might be forgiven,
> He died to make us good,
> That we might go at last to Heaven
> Saved by His precious blood.

She'd sung hymns like that times without number, often had a nice religious feeling as she'd sung them, too, a noble and exalted feeling that was very pleasant while it lasted. The trouble was, it didn't last long. The clergyman's wife, however, made little of feelings, brushing them aside as though they were draperies in front of a window, shutting out the light. Facts were what she was concerned with, and one fact in particular. Jesus Christ was alive today, and He was willing, right here and now, to come into the life of Gladys Aylward, bring her in touch with God, and keep her there. The clergyman's wife seemed very certain about this.

It was all rather stark and unemotional, with no music, no religious atmosphere, no dim lighting, only a draughty room with shabby furniture and the clergyman's wife talking in a matter-of-fact voice about what the Bible said. Gladys, feeling rather upset, sniffed and wiped her nose, her lips tight together, brows furrowed in concentration. She began to realize that she had to make up her mind. It was like standing at the bottom of an escalator, and deciding to get on it, and then getting on it. She had to make up her mind, and then do it.

Eventually she nodded her head, determined and unsmiling. Yes, if God was willing to take her on, she was willing to let Him. So with the clergyman's wife beside her, she knelt down, closed her eyes, and prayed that God would take her on – and as far as she was concerned, she had committed herself for life.

Nothing very dramatic happened. Visits to the theatre fell off, and attendance at gatherings called Young Life Campaigns took their place, with much hymn-singing and extempore prayer and people going up on to the platform and haltingly telling the others what a difference it had made to them since Jesus Christ came into their lives. Queenie was taken along on Sunday afternoons to a hall behind the church, where Gladys rattled away on the piano, and various housemaids of various ages ate bread and butter and cakes after the Bible Class. The lasting impression left on the schoolgirl's mind was that it was a tea-party for old ladies and that Gladys was in charge. If the entertainment value was not, in her estimation, quite up to that provided by a visit to a music hall, or "a seat in the gods at Drury Lane", she made no complaint, for the presence of her cousin was what mattered most to her.

Then Gladys started talking about China.

No one paid any attention to it at first. Apparently she had read a news item in a paper while travelling on a bus, which told of an aeroplane being flown from Shanghai to Lanchow, a city far up the Yellow River in the north-west of China. It was the first time it had happened, and the writer of the article commented on the fact that though this great nation was opening its doors at last to western civilisation, and hospitals, schools, railways, and now even aeroplanes, were appearing, there were still millions of people there who had never heard the Gospel. Something, the writer implied, ought to be done about it.

What all this had to do with Gladys neither Queenie nor her other friends and acquaintances knew. They could not understand why she was continually talking about it, and saying more people ought to go to China as missionaries.

When eventually Dad heard about it he was rather alarmed. He was a quiet man with strong convictions, and Gladys thought the world of him. From time to time young men paid respectful visits to the home and cast a hopeful eye at her, but the affairs always came to nothing. "He's not like Dad," Gladys would say, and that was the end of it. So when he suddenly flared up one day, and scolded her for talking such nonsense about going to China, she was forced to pay attention.

"All this talk about going to China!" he said. "What do you think you're going to do when you get there? Tell me – are you a nurse?"

"No." There was nothing to add to that.

15

"Are you a teacher?"

"No."

"Then what good do you think you'd do in China?"

Dad picked up the newspaper and opened it. He had made his point. He had only one more thing to say, and he said it.

"Go on with you!" he said. "Talk about going to China – talk, talk! That's all you can do – just talk!"

Gladys crept out into the narrow little passage that led to the front door, and stood snivelling at the foot of the stairs. Her father's words were going over and over in her mind, stinging her. "Talk – talk – that's all you can do – just talk!" And then, as she stood there, she stopped crying and found herself whispering, "Talk – talk – *but that's it*!"

# CHAPTER TWO

# The Persistent Call

Gladys had asked for time off. She wanted to keep a very important appointment. It necessitated a forty-minute bus journey from Marble Arch, which took her past King's Cross Station, along Pentonville Road, through a rather down-town shopping centre called the Angel, and landed her eventually at a tree-fringed square around which was built a miscellaneous assortment of shops and houses. At one corner of the square, lying back from the road in a well-kept garden of lawns and shrubberies, was a very large, four-storied building over the doorway of which appeared the words, China Inland Mission and Have Faith in God.

This was just what she wanted – a Mission to go to the inside of China, and faith in God with which to do it. As far as she had been able to ascertain, it was the only missionary society that would be likely to send to China someone like her – someone who was not a nurse, not a teacher, and who had left school at the age of fourteen. She had written to ask if they would take her on, and they had sent her some forms to fill in. She had answered their questions more or less accurately, and now she was coming to meet the Ladies' Council who would then pass on their recommendation to the masculine Candidates'

Committee. Ladies having a voice but no vote, that was the way it was done.

It was in the Minutes of the Candidates' Committee, therefore, that the following item was included on December 12th, 1929:

MISS G. M. AYLWARD – aged 27.10 years of Edmonton, London, was interviewed. Gladys Aylward had been brought up in a Christian home and was converted at eighteen by being brought face to face with her own need as she went from home into business life. She has borne a consistent witness in her place of employment and has worked in the open air and at young people's meetings. In view of the manifest strength of character in this candidate the Ladies' Council recommended one term's testing to see if she is able to settle down to regular study. The Candidates' Committee, after very careful consideration of the case, decided to agree to this recommendation.

So it came about that early in 1930 she entered a tall house known as the Women's Training Home in a cul-de-sac in Highbury, discreetly removed by several blocks from the predominantly masculine headquarters. There were about a couple of dozen trainees that term, most of them younger than she, and they were all on probation. A bell rung at six o'clock each morning had them all out of bed, another bell had them all in the drawing room, Bibles in hand, for morning devotions. They were divided up in shifts for various household chores, and spent hours teaching in local Sunday Schools, preaching in the open air, visiting in the back streets of Hackney.

The highlight of the week was the Wednesday meeting,

held in a large, heavily furnished hall with high windows, and a square platform on which the speakers sat. On the wall beside it hung a huge map of China, sprinkled all over with little red dots, indicating the places where C.I.M. missionaries were located. Reports about their work, information about China generally, talks by people who had actually been there, punctuated by hymn-singing and short prayers, occupied the best part of an hour and a half and when it was all over the young women returned to their Training Home more deeply impressed than ever that their duty and their destiny lay in China.

The warnings that it took over a month to get there, that they would be expected to remain for at least seven years before coming home for their first leave, that they might often be very short of money, without medical help in time of sickness or police protection in times of danger, only served to nerve their endeavour. Even the knowledge that there were two women to every man in the Mission did not deter them. They were prepared to be spinsters to the end of their days if God wanted them in China.

As far as Gladys was concerned, after getting over the initial surprise of finding herself "above stairs" instead of below them with the domestics, she fitted in quite well. She did her household chores with practised efficiency, jumped to the demands of the bells without effort, sang hymns and prayed with the rest of them, and did better than most when it came to visiting dreary homes in back streets, and keeping slum kids in order during Sunday services.

It was the studying and the lectures that baffled her. While the others sat at their desks, listening eagerly, busily taking notes, Gladys sat trying to understand, not knowing what to write in that exercise book in front of her. One of the probationers was a shorthand typist, and after transcribing her notes into long-hand each evening, let Gladys copy them into her own book. This made a good show in the exercise book, but when it came to taking the weekly exam it didn't help at all. The keen eye of the Senior Student, a qualified teacher, soon detected the deficiency, and she put Gladys through her paces, introducing her to the right reference books, asking her questions, explaining the line of reasoning in this, the conclusions to be drawn from that, but all to no avail.

"It just won't go in," said Gladys.

The warden of the Women's Training Home looked apprehensively at those examination papers as they went off to the Candidates' Committee. She was very drawn to Gladys, spoke warmly of her zeal, her ability to get alongside people, especially those who were poor, her promptness in lending a hand when there was a job to be done. She could not deny, however, that when it came to imbibing knowledge by normally accepted methods, Gladys' powers of mental digestion seemed automatically to go into neutral, and occasionally into reverse.

No-one was surprised, with the possible exception of Gladys herself, that at the end of the probationary term she was one of those who was not invited to return for further training. The Chairman of the Committee, a kind-hearted Irishman, pointed out to her gently that unfortunately the Chinese people all spoke Chinese, one of the most difficult languages to learn unless you happened to have been born to it. Months, even years, of painstaking study were required to master it, and her gifts did not appear to lie along the line of study. Her age would make it even more difficult to start now. God had a plan for her life, of that he was sure – possibly here in England. If there was anything he could do to help her . . . Had she any plans as to what she would do when she left the Training Home?

No. No plans. Not now.

The shock of the disappointment was going deep, deeper than she could ever tell. They weren't going to send her to China. She had been so sure she was going to China, so sure God wanted her there, and now she wasn't going.

There was nothing in front of her now, nothing. She had no plans.

"While you're looking round for something suitable, would you like to help two missionaries who are back in this country now? They need some help. . . ."

So she went to Bristol to the missionary couple, and with calm simplicity they told her about their experiences through life, and how God had helped them.

"God never lets you down – never. He'll guide you. He'll provide for you, too. Trust Him. He'll show you what He wants you to do." They gave her a little card with "Be not afraid, remember the Lord" on it. She kept it in her Bible.

In the months that followed she tried to find out what it was God wanted her to do. She went as helper for a few weeks in a hostel for working women, then she stayed with people she had known in London who were working among down-and-outs in Swansea, then she took a job as Assistant Matron in what was known as the Sunshine Hostel, where girls were taken in who needed a night's lodging. In some cases they needed it more than they wanted it, as Gladys discovered when she went looking for them down on the streets near the docks where the sailors came swaggering along from their ships, money jingling in their pockets. One way and another she saw life in the raw those months in Swansea, when the trade slump was bringing unemployment, dole, queues, desperate poverty in its train. Families were living by their dozens in derelict rat-infested houses, children half naked, women filthy, men degraded – she had never seen anything like it before.

"We can't let them be like this!" she exclaimed, and recklessly giving away all the clothes she could lay her hands on, wrote to her family demanding some of theirs, too. When she got people cleaned up and clothed, she insisted on them coming with her to the Gospel Mission to hear about God. They'd got souls as well as bodies to be saved, she pointed out with passionate insistence. She'd done what she could about their bodies, now let God have a chance to do what He could with their souls.

"You're doing a grand work here," people assured her. "This is the right place for you!" But in spite of everything they said, Gladys knew that it wasn't.

"I can't explain why," she had told Queenie. "But somehow I know its got to be China."

She knew it as surely as Abraham knew he had to get out of Ur of the Chaldees, or Moses that he had to go to Egypt to fetch those Israelites. China it had to be. If no-one would send her she'd pay her own fare and she'd buy a ticket and go to China. She'd go back to parlourmaiding therefore, and she'd save her money and she'd buy a ticket and go to China. So the day came when she found herself back in London sitting on the edge of a narrow bed in a little room with a china jug and basin on a wash-stand and not much else, once more in domestic service. Beside her was her Bible, and her Daily Light and a few coppers – all the money she possessed in the world. She put them together, placed her hand on them, and closed her eyes tightly.

A quarter of a century later when Gladys Aylward's story was being glamourized in the film "Inn of The Sixth Happiness", this incident was retained almost as it must have happened. There was a reality and a simplicity about it that defied the touch of the most skilful artist to improve it, and Ingrid Bergman, the actress who took the part of Gladys, admitted that this was the scene which moved her more deeply than any other. For the London parlourmaid, almost in tears, at the end of her resources and nearly thirty years of age now, prayed with passionate earnestness.

"Oh, God! Here's me. Here's my Bible, here's my money! Use us, God! Use us!"

She heard a voice calling her name. It was only one of the other maids, with a message that the mistress wanted to see her. She wiped her nose, hastily adjusted her cap, and sped downstairs. The mistress had merely summoned her because, as she explained, it was her practice to pay the fares of her maids when she engaged them. How much had it cost Gladys to come to Belgrave Square from Edmonton?

When Gladys remounted the stairs she held 3/- in her hand, ten times the amount she had placed on her Bible and as far as she was concerned it had come straight from God towards her fare to China. And if He could multiply

23

what she gave Him as quickly as that, she'd be there sooner than she had expected!

From that time things went smoothly. She worked on her half-days and sometimes through the night, helping at parties in other houses, and saved every penny she earned. She went to shipping offices to find out how to get to China, and learned that the cheapest and quickest way, though by no means the most comfortable or safest, was to go by railway through Europe, Russia and Siberia.

She did not know what she would do when she got to Tientsin, or where she would go from there, but after a time that problem was solved, too. She went one evening to a meeting, and someone said to her,

"I've got a friend who's got a friend who has just gone to China. Her name is Mrs. Lawson. She is seventy-three and has been a missionary in China for years. She came home, but she couldn't settle, so she's gone out again. She's praying for some young person to go out and join her ..."

"That's me," said Gladys.

She went to a travel agent and ordered a single, one-way ticket, third class to Tientsin, and persuaded him to receive the money for it in advance in small instalments until the necessary sum of £47 10s. had been paid, so that she wouldn't be tempted to give it away.

On Saturday, 15th October, 1932, she set off from Liverpool Street Station to go to China – to fulfil her destiny.

# CHAPTER THREE

# Journey to China

She set off on that journey in a reefer coat, an orange frock that had belonged to Mum, a cap-like hat made by Vi, carrying a couple of suitcases, one filled with food, a roll of bedding, and a brown bag containing a spirit stove, kettle and saucepan tied together with a piece of string. In her corset, which was obviously the safest place, Mum had made neat little pockets to contain her passport, fountain pen, some travellers' cheques and a small Bible. If some emergency separated her from her luggage, only a catastrophe of the most unspeakable type could separate her from these essentials.

A group of friends and Mum and Vi were there at Liverpool Street Station to see her off. Dad had travelled with them part of the way from Edmonton, but left them at Bethnal Green, because he couldn't be late for work, he said.

They all understood. They knew he could not bear to stand on the platform waiting for the whistle to blow, waiting for Gladys to get on the train and sit looking out at them with those big dark eyes of hers, seeing her trying not to cry as she set out to go, alone, to China. A day's trip to the Isle of Wight was the farthest she had ever been from England's shores, and now she was embarking on an expedition that would take three weeks by train, always assuming that everything went well when she got to the border of Manchuria, where there was a war on. Dad could not face that last half-hour. He got off the train, his eyes sharp with pain, and Gladys looked at him and just said, "Goodbye, Dad," and stood at the carriage door watching him as the train pulled out, on towards Liverpool Street.

There was the usual hustle and bustle at the main line station where the Cross Channel train was drawn up, with porters trundling trunks and suitcases along the platform, sophisticated-looking, elegant passengers sweeping into the First Class compartments, and shabbier ones carrying their own boxes and bundles into those marked Third. Little groups of people stood talking and laughing, here and there women whose eyes were red with weeping tried to force a smile, the whistle blew, passengers hurried into the train, doors slammed, the guard waved his flag.

"Goodbye, Gladys!"

"Goodbye Glad – God bless you."

"Goodbye Vi – Goodbye, Mum – Goodbye . . ." She stood at the window, waving to them until they were out of sight . . .

Everything went well at first. She wrote her impressions on a big writing pad, so that she could tear out the pages and send them home whenever she got to a place where she could post them. With characteristic disregard for the hampering rules of grammar and punctuation, she wrote as she talked, relating all that happened.

"The Dutch boys are wonderful they were all lined up on the landing stage, and each passenger who needs a porter is given a number, and when they get to the Custom House they just look for their number, mine was

26

thirty-one, so when I came off the boat, I just looked for thirty-one, who had all my bags up on the counter.

"They did not open them, they just signed the paper, and away I went to the train, I gave him a shilling in English money, and he was very pleased. The police in Holland are very smart, but the porters here are smarter in their way, they have a strap round them, and just hook all the bags etc. round, and you can hardly see some of them for bags."

When she got on the train for Berlin, two of the other passengers got in after her, well-dressed, obviously husband and wife. The woman glanced at Gladys, then a look of recognition came into her eyes, and she smiled.

"Why, here is the little girl who had all the people to see her off from London," she said.

"Did you come from London?" responded Gladys. The lady sat beside her and continued talking.

"And where are you going?" she enquired kindly.

"I'm going to China," Gladys replied.

"You're going – *where*?"

"I'm going to China."

"Oh! What a long way. Is your young man there?"

"No."

"Oh! Aren't you going to China to get married?"

"No."

"What are you going there for, then?" asked the lady, rather surprised.

"I'm going to China to preach the Gospel," Gladys said definitely, and the lady was even more surprised. She had met missionaries before, but none like this one, and as Gladys chatted away, her interest deepened. They talked together until the train drew up at the station where the couple were to get off. "We shall meet again," said the lady with significant earnestness as she kissed Gladys goodbye. Gladys knew what she meant, of course. They would meet again in Heaven if not before, and she nodded emphatically. Gladys reported on her writing pad,

". . . they were lovely, and we had Prayer before they got out, and I was left with a Schofield Testament, and £1 in English money."

After they had gone Gladys had a little difficulty with the ticket collector who came along the train. He could not speak English, and she could speak nothing else, and the conversation that ensued attracted the attention of a German girl in the next compartment.

"She came in to settle him, well again we talked, and here I am in her home. She would not hear of me staying on the station, and when I have finished writing this we are going to see a little of Berlin. Hasn't God been good to me, I have had no bother with my luggage which is now in the cloak room at the station. . . . The trains here run *overhead* not *underground*, and the police just stand like statues they wear long capes, and are armed with a little bayonet arrangement. Everything here is very clean and orderly, but not a bit like England."

She boards a train bound for Moscow, and her only companion in the compartment is a Polish man. Efforts at conversation include much wagging of heads, waving of hands, and laughter, and as far as officials are concerned "I have had no bother yet because I cannot understand what they say to me so I just shake my head." As they leave Warsaw, and speed on towards Russia, however, she notices that everywhere are soldiers on guard.

"It seems so strange to us who are used to freedom, they get into the train, and look under the seats, and behind the curtains. They are very polite to me, and bow and diddle diddle Madame, they wear Russian boots, and look very smart in Air Force Blue with red tops to their hats. . . . My Polish companion is at this moment snoring very loudly and the train is rocking a little so my thoughts are a little disconnected, we have had one more talk with hands and heads, and he gave me an apple, so I have lent him my grey rug." It was he who gave her the stamp for her letter, and went with her to post it before they eventually parted company and she was left alone in her compartment.

The train rattles on, and so does Gladys. Dad was right, they do run these trains on wood. She smelt it burning and went in the corridor to see, and the engine driver showed her all over the engine. They arrive at the Russian border, and she is very happy "since China is now nearly in sight", although what she sees of Russia makes her thankful to God she was born English! She has just had her dinner, boiled egg, Ryvita and a cup of tea. "I had an Oxo at 11 o'clock my little stove is wonderful and my saucepan is better than my kettle for boiling although I use the kettle for fetching my water in. . . . I have not yet started on Auntie Bessie's cake but am going to start it for my tea today."

As the journey continues and water is more difficult to obtain, she sprints along the platform when the train stops, to the tap where the other passengers rush to fill their pots and their buckets. Her orange frock attracts much interest!

She arrives at Moscow, where she must change trains,

and she notices many soldiers, untidy-looking, down-at-heel dirty men who carry bread under their arms and pull off lumps and walk along eating it. There is something rather ominous about the atmosphere of Moscow that obviously affects her, but she cheers up again once she is on a train heading towards China. She has to share a compartment with three men, but they are very polite.

"I was not a bit nervous I curled my hair put on my smart cap said my prayers and went off sound to sleep we all got up about seven-thirty because we stopped for water, a nice young man went and filled my kettle for me." The train chugs on, across the silent and lonely steppes, and on the fourth day she wakes feeling sad and weeps a little, until she opens her Bible at one of the Psalms, and after reading it feels better. The scenery stirs her deeply, and she describes the deep red glow in the sky which stretches right over the black clouds and makes it all look like a golden sea. She observes the animals, too, big black dogs with shaggy coats and long tails, and at night little wild things that "look like cats but go into the ground like rabbits."

She feels happy, so sings "I walk with the King, Hallelujah!" and the people in the carriage smile. They seem to like it very much, though they cannot understand what it is all about. It is Sunday, as it happens, and a man gets in who can speak a little English, and at last there is someone to talk to! The carriage fairly buzzes with conversation, for everybody wants to know about her, and he acts as interpreter.

Before he gets out, however, he passes on to her a disturbing message. It is from the conductor. He wants her to know that there are now no trains running to Harbin, because of the fighting, and therefore she may be held up at the border.

"This of course worried me very much," wrote Gladys the following day, "and I went to bed quite forgetting to have any supper and I lay for some time hardly knowing what to do. Then I thought, I am failing God, so I found my little Bible, and I thought, I will read my favourite part in the Old Testament the deliverance of the Children of Israel how God brought all those millions of people out of bondage. Well when I opened my Bible out dropped a piece of paper and on it were these words, 'Be not afraid, remember the Lord,' which was given to me when in Bristol. It was too much for me, I just cried, here was I worrying, when in Heaven was God helping me all along . . . I would not if I could turn back now because I believe that God is going to reveal Himself in a wonderful way."

After that she did not write anything on her writing pad for a week. It was the most terrifying week she had ever lived through, and from the comparative comfort and apparent security of the Intourist Hotel in the port of Vladivostok she continued her Pepys-like record to send to the family in Edmonton. She explained how a man had been sent to warn her it was dangerous to go on, but she had not understood, so when all the other passengers except soldiers descended onto the platform, she sat tight in the train.

"On we went but the fighting was right on the line so the train went back and at the first stop they made me get out." She did not tell them she had to carry all her things, trudging alone along the railway track thick with snow, back to Chita. She did not want to worry them. . . .

"Well, I humped my baggage along to the middle of the platform and sat on it feeling very dazed, I had two cases, the bed done up in the grey blanket, my two rugs, my handbag and brown bag with saucepan, stove and kettle inside, my shoes tied together to the handle also two coats on. You see I had no time to pack properly, my kettle had water in it so it had to be kept upright. So there I sat, it was very cold I was hungry and very uncomfortable just hanging on to my things because all the people crowded round me trying to steal them" she wrote, and then she added, "But they did not manage it!"

As she sat there like a lonely little sparrow among the crows, cold and frightened, she found herself saying "Oh, God, was it worth this?"

"... and to my mind like a flash came 'Be not afraid, remember the Lord', so I prayed that God would remember me and deliver me. I believe He did but in quite a different way to what I imagined."

No spectacular deliverance occurred during the nightmareish days and nights that followed, but they were punctuated by apparently irrelevant inspirations which led her through the maze. The first one came right there on the platform.

"It came to me that if I made a commotion and got *arrested* something would have to be done for me (you can imagine me making it!) well I did, and along came a soldier to move me on, but there I sat. Well three came in turn and then along came a very tall official one with a red hat on and with three others. Off I was marched, I went very quietly with my baggage without which I would not move, and put into a place so filthy oh dear I have never seen anything like it. The smell was horrible, I thought I should faint, so I brought out my passport to show that I was British so they railed me off from the others, and there I was ..."

As the others were mainly men, several hundred of them, of various nationalities and very rough-looking, that separation under guard was a God-send, though Gladys wrote that she nearly died with fright.

"Then all at once I saw Auntie Bessie and she had in her hand a green card and said, 'Remember the Lord, He is with thee.' That vision was very clear and I was at peace for I knew that my God was guarding me even in that horrible place."

Meanwhile, the officials themselves were not without their problems. Here was a fiery-eyed little creature in an orange frock with a strange assortment of possessions from which she refused to be separated, who talked to them in staccato sentences which they could not understand, whose official papers indicated she was on a one-way journey to China, but who had got off a train which was clearly travelling in the opposite direction. If they mistook her for a fugitive from justice, it would not have been surprising. Her profession, according to the passport, was "missionary", and what they made of that was that she was in some way connected with machinery. They were in the process of trying to explain to her that there was plenty of scope for people with a knowledge of machinery in Russia, when she had another of her inspirations.

"... the interpreter said evidently I was something to do with machines and they were trying to persuade me to stop in Russia as I was useful to them. When this dawned on me I did not know what to do. How I prayed and how near God seemed, so with boldness I fetched out my Bible and with a little picture Helene sent me from Germany I explained what I was. That did it, things moved then. Before I knew where I was I had a new visa, another ticket had been made out for me, then I was taken all round Chita to see it and impress me with Russia, then I was put in a train." Instructions were given her where to change for Harbin, but when she got off the train it was to learn that the Japanese had closed in, and the line was blocked. "Go to Vladivostok!" she was told. The first train was so crowded she could not struggle on, but she fought her way onto the next, and eventually landed at the great port in north-east Asia, on the Sea of Japan.

Again no one could understand her, and she had to spend the night on the station platform, shivering with cold.

"But in the morning I went to the Government Office having put my luggage into the cloakroom without paying for it, there I thought somebody will speak English, but no."

Then it was that she had another of those irrelevant inspirations. She was nearly in tears by this time, and perhaps it was partly for her own comfort that she produced a picture of her soldier brother. When the officials saw it the tide turned immediately in her favour. "They at once thought he was an officer in the British Army, (he is so smart and well dressed compared to their soldiers) I don't know what they said but they got my luggage from the station and sent me with an escort to this hotel. Can you imagine my joy to hear English again and to be able to rest. I have slept in a bed, the first time since I left home also I have been able to have a proper wash, oh the joy to be clean, this is the first time I have had my clothes off since I left home."

That letter was written on Monday, October 31st, and ended with the words,

"I thought I knew the value of prayer before but never as now. When everything seemed against me He was there ready to help me over the difficult places and now here I am safe and happy just waiting to go on and would willingly go through it all again for the joy of knowing my Saviour as I know Him now."

What happened shortly after writing that, she did not commit to paper. The next entry in her diary-letters was five days later, from Kobe in Japan, and commenced simply,

"God has been good to me, but I could not get a connection from Russia to Harbin so had to come by steamer from Vladivostok to Tsuruga and thence here." She did not mention the sinister way the official looked at her as he tried to persuade her to stay and work in Russian territory. Nor did she tell of the young woman who had sidled up beside her when no one was looking, and whispered urgently in broken English that she must get away that night or she would never get away at all. She didn't want to get Mum worried by relating the terrifying experience of the man who appeared at her bedroom door, his one intention all too evident, and who had so perplexedly backed away as she spat out defiantly, "You can't touch me! God won't let you!" And even if she had escaped from the Intourist hotel at midnight, with the help of that unknown woman who had warned her of her danger, and had been taken on to a Japanese boat after signing

35

some papers, and thus landed in Japan instead of China, it was all over now! Being British had ensured the help of the Consul, and now here she was at the Japan Evangelistic Band Mission Home, where everybody was very kind, and ready to help her in any way possible to get to her destination.

She was charmed with Japan, with its snow-covered mountains, pretty houses with quaint roofs, colourful fruit and flowers – "it seems like Heaven after the desolateness of Russia." She had a bath in a large wooden tub "in which you boil, but was very refreshing," and slept in a little white bed with a blue cover, and a red and blue lantern hanging from the ceiling.

Altogether, everything was lovely. The only little worry she had was that her orange dress was now very, very dirty, and when her shoes had been removed, Japanese fashion, everyone could see that one of her stockings had a hole in it.

# CHAPTER FOUR

# The Inn in Yangcheng

North of the Yellow River, in the province of Shansi, West of the Mountains, lay the city of Tsechow. For centuries strings of camels had come padding through it on the old trade route leading towards central China, along with mules and donkeys, and coolies swinging slowly along with their loads on carrying-poles. Now, in 1932, an occasional four-wheeled mechanical monster roared and snorted its way along the main street, to come to a halt in the pot-holed road surrounded by swarms of men and children who stood and gazed with expressionless faces at the passengers as they alighted.

On November 16, Gladys was one of these.

She was still wearing her orange frock and her blue reefer coat, and was accompanied by a young man named Mr. Lu, who had been sent to Tientsin to escort her to her destination. The boat journey from Japan to China had been without incident, the welcome in the London Missionary Society home in Tientsin warm and friendly, but she had been five days on the road since then, travelling deeper and deeper into the mountains, the object of that expressionless gaze of Chinese who seemed to appear from nowhere as soon as she arrived. It had been a relief to discover that there were missionaries in two of the towns on the way, and to go into their clean secluded homes for a few hours to enjoy the *camaraderie* that exists between exiles. Now she had arrived at the headquarters of the tiny Mission to which Mrs. Lawson was loosely attached, a place she was to visit many times in the years that lay ahead.

The first missionary to live in Tsechow was a Cambridge undergraduate named Stanley Smith, who had come to China towards the end of the nineteenth century, along with six other young men from the higher strata of English society. They were known as the Cambridge Seven, and scattered far and wide in the Imperial Chinese Empire, wearing Chinese clothes, eating Chinese food, living in Chinese houses, and proclaiming the news of eternal salvation through Jesus Christ the Lord in the best Chinese they could muster.

Stanley Smith had settled in Tsechow, and travelled out from it steadily and patiently, establishing four other centres over an area about half the size of Wales, and even more mountainous, before he died. In Tsechow itself was a church and a boarding school for the children of Christians. In the other centres there was little more than a compound with some dwelling places for missionaries (if there were missionaries to live in them) and Chinese helpers.

The Mission compound in Tsechow, therefore, was quite a hub, presided over by Stanley Smith's widow, a charming old lady who after nearly half a century among the illiterate peasants of West of the Mountains had never quite shaken off the culture of the society into which she had been born. She could no more help being the niece of an Archbishop to the end of her days than Gladys could help being a London parlourmaid to the end of hers! But although she was the sort of person Gladys was accustomed to taking orders from and calling "Madam", there was no consciousness of social distinctions at that first meeting. Gladys wrote enthusiastically,

"... oh, what a welcome I had! It was lovely.... I feel that Mrs. Smith is going to be my mother out here, I love her already...."

She was quite sorry to leave Tsechow, but Mr. Lu was all for pressing on, so after a couple of days they set off on the last lap of the journey. Gladys was no longer wearing her orange frock. Mrs. Smith had supplied her with the attire of a Chinese country woman, wadded trousers and jacket, explaining,

"We missionaries all wear Chinese clothes. We want to be as like the Chinese as possible – and their clothes are much more sensible than ours, anyway!"

She travelled by mule litter over the mountain ranges until, in the distance, she saw a walled city set on the side of a hill. It was Yangcheng, Mr. Lu told her. She looked at it with relief. She was very tired, and very sore from the continual rub of the net seat that was strung between the mules, in which she was being jerked up and down, so it was difficult to produce any very lofty reactions.

"Our journey took us two days and I thought I should be all broken in little pieces before I arrived, but when we reached Yangcheng and found my arms and legs were still where they should be I thanked God for all his goodness to me. Mrs. Lawson also was very pleased to see me and many of the Mission people called to tell me how very glad they were that I had arrived safely."

She did not mention that the Mission compound at Yangcheng was utterly different from any of the others

she had seen, with its dilapidated buildings, its heaps of
rubble, its buckets and its brooms left around in the courtyard and general air of neglect and untidiness. She drew
a veil over the coolness of the reception she got from
Jeannie Lawson, with her mop of white hair crowning
five feet of Scottish skin and bones, who snapped when
she saw her,

"Well, and who are you?" as though she were a gipsy
who had turned up at the back door. The old lady was
seventy-three and somewhat bewildered, and had probably forgotten she had sent her evangelist to Tientsin to
escort a young woman she had never met to come and live
with her for the rest of her life! When Gladys explained
that she had written to her from London, the other just
nodded and said,

"Well, do you want to come in?"

Jeannie Lawson was wonderful – once you got used
to her. She had come back to China to die there, and she
was determined to die "in harness". She took Gladys
out, introducing her to the people of Yangcheng, and
taught her a few sentences which Gladys reproduced
fairly accurately, to bring out when she was spoken to,
laughing and cheerful. And since Gladys must have a
name, and the Chinese could not be expected to pro-
nounce Aylward, she was called Ai Weh Teh instead, as
the nearest that could be got to it. She translated it for
the folk at home as best she could. It meant The Virtuous
One.

It was Mrs. Lawson who conceived the fantastic idea
of turning their courtyard into an inn, so that some of the
muleteers who travelled across the mountains could turn

in there, and thus give her the opportunity of telling them of Jesus Christ. To Gladys fell the task of persuading them that it was a good place to come to, and very apprehensively she stood at the double-leaved gates of the compound, ready to grab the bridle of the first mule in the train and lead him in, while she called out to the muleteers,

"We have no fleas! We have no bugs!" She learned this from the cook, who assured her it was the correct approach. Had she paused for reflection, she might have questioned the validity of the claim, but Gladys was not given to reflection.

"No fleas! No bugs! Good! Good! Come! Come!" she called in Chinese with a strong Cockney accent, and leapt into the fray. It was a hazardous undertaking, especially for a Londoner who had never ridden anything more lively than a donkey on the sands at Margate, for the mules were big and could be very nasty. She decided not to mention it in her letters home. Mum might worry. And that bit about the fleas and the bugs.... No, better say nothing about it.

In any case, it was only part of the day's work, and it didn't happen every day. It was learning Chinese that had to happen every day, and she had to do it alone. Other young missionaries started with their books and their trained teachers, in a well-equipped language school, and only after several months' organised instruction were they sent out to live among the Chinese. It was a method that would have been intolerable for Gladys, with her restless active nature and dislike of study. As it was, she applied herself to books for short periods, but when she

41

was tired dropped them and went out to see what was
happening in the streets of Yangcheng.

"... Even if I just go down the road I have a crowd of
children. If I go to a shop I have to go to the best room
and take tea, and then they serve me. I take a small boy
with me, and never go alone," she wrote, and went on,
"The language is very difficult, but I am a good mimic
and so am picking up little bits without study."

So commenced her missionary career, and so she
picked up, with remarkable accuracy, the language she
could probably never have learned in any other way. So,
also, she started to develop the independent spirit that
was to carry her far beyond the spheres in which the aver-
age missionary moves. There were times when the dour
determined old Scot, and the quick determined young
Londoner clashed, and on at least one such occasion
Gladys was told to get out!

Tearful but defiant she did so.

For a few weeks she lived with missionaries in a city
represented by one of those red dots on that big map in
the China Inland Mission headquarters in London. She
stayed with Dr. and Mrs. Stanley Hoyte, who had several
children, and as Mrs. Hoyte had to go to Peking for an
operation it was arranged that Gladys should act as
nanny to them in her absence. However, while she was
away news came through that Mrs. Lawson was ill, and
Gladys was off like a shot, back to Yangcheng. Dr. Hoyte
took it philosophically,

"She believed that God had told her to leave the Hoyte
children and go to Mrs. Lawson, so she left them, although I had to be away two days to bring my wife

42

home," he wrote, and added that as for the children, "They came to no harm. The servants looked after them."

But Mrs. Lawson died. And with her, the income that had supported the Mission in Yangcheng.

# CHAPTER FIVE

# *Inspector of Feet*

It was mainly a matter of feet, where marriages were concerned. A pretty face, fair skin, a strong healthy body were all very well in their way, but it was the feet that could make or break it when it came to finding a suitable husband for your daughter. There was something exclusive about feet, something that set them apart from the rest of the body as being a sort of status symbol; the smaller a girl's feet, the more delicately she tottered on little stumps that resembled goats' hoofs, the clearer the evidence that she had been properly brought up in a genteel family, and was fit to be the first wife of an eligible son in an equally genteel family. For centuries mothers in China had looked anxiously at the feet of their daughters, bound tight from babyhood, toes crushed under, and hardened their hearts against cries and whimpers as they pulled the bandages more firmly, muttering,

"It's no use crying. How shall we ever find a husband for you, with these great feet?" And the little girls, as they grew older, looked down at their own feet, comparing them with the feet of their companions, and submitting to any treatment that would prevent them from getting bigger. Men wanted wives with small feet, and that was that!

The reason for this lay far back in history when, so it

was said, one of the wives of the Emperor had escaped from the palace and run away. This, of course, reflected badly on His Imperial Majesty, and set a very bad example to all women in the Empire. If wives and concubines were free to take to their heels and make a dash for it whenever there was a slight domestic upset, where would the thing end? Women being what they were, and nature having so disposed matters that the sexes were equally divided, in no time at all half the population of the country might be running away from the other half! Even if it did not come to that, the dignity and authority of the male was in danger of toppling, and something must be done to set him firmly on his base again. Women must be permanently prevented from running away, and the simple solution to the whole problem lay in their feet.

And so, for several centuries the feet of baby girls in China were so dealt with that never in their lives could they run.

With the overthrow of the Ch'ing Dynasty in 1912 and the establishment of the Republic of China things began to change. The queues of the men, ancient symbol of servitude to the Manchu Emperors, must go. So must the custom of foot-binding. Twenty years later it was hard to find any men, other than old Taoist priests, who sported queues. However reluctant they had been at first to part with those long plaits of glossy hair hanging from their crowns they had soon got used to being without them.

It was a different matter when it came to the women's feet. The new law might have been successfully enforced in the cities and towns on the coast and on the main lines of communication, but away from them, back in the mountains and the vast agricultural plains, in the little walled villages where women rarely went beyond the confines of their own courtyards, small feet were still a status symbol. But now the Government was determined that they must go. The decree had gone forth, and it had reached, among other places, the city of Yangcheng. Footbinding must be abolished, completely and utterly, and the magistrates of areas where it was still practised were put on their mettle. It was up to them to see that it was done away with.

This was easier said than done, for it involved *seeing* that it was done, and here the female foot presented another problem. As everybody knew, the female foot must not be seen unclothed, not even when it was being washed. How then could a man be submitted to the indignity of having to demand to see the naked foot of a woman to ensure that it was free of the evidences of footbinding? Only a woman could be told to do that, and the magistrate of Yangcheng, after much thought and consultation came to the conclusion that the most suitable woman in the whole city to take on the job of official Inspector of Feet was Ai Weh Teh.

Once she got over the shock of it, Gladys reacted to the suggestion with enthusiasm. Here was something to write home about! The family in Edmonton might not have seen the funny side of the mules, the fleas and the bugs, and now that Mrs. Lawson had died and the inn was no longer functioning she had forgotten all about it. But they would be tickled to death at the idea of her being official Inspector of Feet! What an opening for the preaching of the Gospel, and all at the expense of the Government! She was to be the recipient of a daily ration of grain, would be provided with a bodyguard of two soldiers who would be at hand to enforce her commands, and a mule on which to ride when she sallied forth to the villages. Armed with the authority of the magistrate, she could go into any home, demand to see the women and girls, sit down and talk to them, say what she liked so long as she made them finish with foot-binding.

Generations of missionaries, all over China, had waged a wordy war against the evils of foot-binding, but it is doubtful whether any of them had a better opportunity of wiping it out than had Gladys as a young missionary alone in Yangcheng. And by the time she relinquished her position, and Ru Mai a young Chinese widow with three children took it on instead, she was a familiar figure throughout the countryside, whither she went off from village to village for weeks at a time, her bedding and boxes of Gospels and tracts piled on a cart.

"We put up for nights where we can. Sometimes it is clean sometimes not. All depends! but we talk, sing and pray all the time." And when she was in Yangcheng it was the same. She was up and down the streets, into the court-yards where women sat spinning thread or winnowing grain, quick, cheerful, interested in what they were doing, learning to do it herself, and then squatting down beside them to talk. To talk.

It was there among the peasants of Shansi that she learned by experience the art that was to bring her into the limelight on a very different stage from that at which she looked so longingly from her seat "in the gods at Drury Lane". It was in those lonely years that she developed, quite unconsciously, the skill of the true story-teller. With her own limited Chinese vocabulary and her listeners' limited knowledge of the outside world she had to convey messages from the Living God in a way they could understand. Away with cluttering details and accurate, deadly facts! Like a lightning artist, in vivid, bald, intimate sentences she depicted the children of Israel pouring out of Egypt, and they were all Chinese, with their carrying poles, and their babies bobbing up and down in baskets, their wadded quilts and their bags of grain, their shallow cooking pans and their bowls and chopsticks.

It was outside the wall of Yangcheng that they saw a patient young Peasant nailed to a cross, hanging there in the blazing heat of the north China sun, the flies buzzing about his head, two criminals shrieking on crosses beside him. It was in the guttering light from an oil lamp in one of their own rooms that they saw Him alive again, holding out His hands to show them the scars left by the nails in proof that it was He.

And let it be known to the people of Yangcheng that He was alive today! She knew, for He had spoken to her. Yes, it was to her, Ai Weh Teh, she who sat before them now, that He had spoken when she was in her own country, telling her to get out and come and live among them. And as she told them of the way that call had come, the drama of it gripped her afresh, and as she related the story of that terrible journey and the way God was with her through it all, her own eyes glowed and her listeners held their breath. An awesome awareness of a Presence stole over them, and they knew that what she was telling them was real.

She did not confine herself to the streets, either. There was a prison in Yangcheng, and she found her way in there.

"The prison work is going on. The change in that place is remarkable and I am full of praise. . . . I don't know whether I told you of the girl in the prison. She is only twenty and has already been in two years. Her sentence is fifteen years for killing her husband, but she has come right out for God and is giving a real bright witness in there. Everybody says there is a difference. . . . Then four men have also really believed. . . ."

Ai Weh Teh became a person to be reckoned with, both in Yangcheng and Tsechow. When David and Jean Davies arrived as new missionaries in Tsechow, the first person to welcome them was Gladys, her black hair combed straight back to form a bun at the back of her head, wearing a simple cotton Chinese gown. She had come along with a deputation of the church elders, and was waiting for them at the city gate. It was she who had all the children in the school lined up, ready to sing a welcome. She knew how to organise those children, did Gladys! The Davies' were filled with admiration for this small but forceful young woman who seemed to understand everything the Chinese said and who, sometimes to their amused alarm, did everything the Chinese did. She could spit with the best of them, and when she bit on a piece of gristle at a feast it shot out of her mouth with the utmost precision to where the dog under the table was waiting to snap it up.

The Chinese adored her, David Davies noticed. "She's one with us," they told him, although the church elders wagged their heads sometimes over her generosity, and David went farther and wagged his tongue, telling her that people were taking advantage of her. The elders had told him that she was encouraging the wrong sort of people to come round the church by giving things away so freely. She listened, pursing her lips and nodding her head, and said she'd make enquiries about people before helping them. But her good intentions never lasted long. The false as well as the true knew where they could get free board and lodging, although they soon discovered she was as sharp as a needle over some things. "They needn't think they can pinch my things!" she said as she glanced round to ensure that her wadded quilt, her comb, her towel and her face basin were where she had left them. And she knew just how little she could get it for when it came to driving a bargain in the market.

Those were sunlit years in Shansi, the model province West of the Mountains, as many a time she rode off on a mule to the villages, or to stay for a while with the Davies's in Tsechow. The Eighth Route Army with Chu Teh and Mao Tse Tung in its ranks was marching to settle in Yenan, like a lion crouching in its lair waiting for the moment to spring, and the Japanese were massing their troops on the Manchurian borders, but she gave not a thought to them, if, indeed, she knew of their existence. She was solely concerned with the present. Travelling was primitive and tedious but comparatively safe, for the bandits were of the gentlemanly variety, for whom highway robbery was merely a productive little side line to be pursued when things were slack on the farm. Living was cheap, and she subsisted without difficulty on money gifts that came to her from time to time, some from England, some from missionaries who knew her circumstances.

She was lonely, it is true. The self-revelations which endeared her to thousands in later years told of her prayers for a husband, and how she looked for the answer, expecting to see a Prince Charming walking towards her over the mountains – "But he never came." Then she hoped for a woman companion, and excitement rose when she received a letter from "Evelyn" who wanted to join her. Gladys could not remember who she was but,

". . . that does not make any difference when we are about the Lord's business, so I will try to answer your questions," wrote she, and proceeded to fill both sides of five sheets of paper.

"Before I begin to tell you of actual things may I just say first, that if God has called you to China or any other place and you are sure in your own heart, let nothing deter you . . . remember it is God who has called you and it is the same as when He called Moses or Samuel."

She tells of her own experiences, of people trying to discourage her from going forward, and of her own effort to escape that inward conviction, but "the urge was still there and I found nothing would do but go. I have lived in China now for over three years, and I have never asked anyone for a penny and yet God has supplied my every need."

She eagerly goes through all her belongings, discovers she has sheets, pillow cases and towels enough for two, and goes out and buys a bed and a mosquito net in anticipation of Evelyn's coming,

"So make haste and come. Don't be too long for the time is short. And one thing more, I do not want you to think I am an old fussy creature and will want to boss you, you will be quite free only I must mother you a bit. You will let me won't you? How I have dreamt of getting you some pretty Chinese clothes. . . ."

But the next letter from Evelyn reveals she is still in her teens, and even Gladys realises that this is too young, so she does not come, either.

The longing for someone to mother does not remain unsatisfied however, for right on her doorstep are little unwanted children needing just what she has to give. She sees a hard-faced woman by the roadside, and discovers with hot indignation that the pitiable, wizened, wild-looking creature with her is a small girl up for sale. Furious, Gladys goes to the magistrate to report, but he shrugs his shoulders. There has always been a quiet traffic in women-children, and it is better not to interfere. It might prove very dangerous, for the people behind the traffic are very powerful. Ai Weh Teh is instructed to pass by on the other side.

But this she cannot do. In the end, since there is no other way of saving the child, she buys it herself – for ninepence. After all, it is only one more little mouth to feed, along with the gatekeeper, and the woman servant, and Ru Mai's two children who are always in and out. So Ninepence, as she was nicknamed, came to stay, and after that Gladys had no cause to feel lonely, for she was only the first of a long stream of little children who needed to be mothered.

Meanwhile, although the people of Yangcheng had accepted her and she moved in and out freely among them, she knew there was something different about herself. She was still not really one of them. "Why is it?" she asked herself, searching for the reason. As she faced her own question she realised that at heart she was still British. She had not renounced her national pride, and determined that this also must go. So she took a step which was ultimately to sever for ever any legal claim she had on the country of her birth. It was one that was to have far-reaching consequences that she could not have foreseen, although it would not have made any difference to the action she took. It was something she felt God wanted her to do, so she did it.

She destroyed her British passport, and applied to become a naturalised Chinese.

# CHAPTER SIX

# War in the Mountains

It was in July, 1937, that a shot fired across a river triggered off the Japanese undeclared war against China, unleashing a stream of misery and suffering that was to affect millions of people, sweeping Gladys along with it. In the early months, however, it disturbed her not at all except that the weeks and then the months passed by, and still no letters reached her from home, so when at last one came through and she recognised her mother's handwriting, "I could not open it the tears came and my hands trembled, for the joy seemed more than I could bear." Even when rumours ran through the city like an electric shock, telling of Japanese advancing towards Luan in the north, she was too busy with her visiting and her journeys to the villages, her classes in the prison and the children on the compound to give much thought to them. Life was full and happy until one morning in the Spring of 1938, she and the evangelist and Ru Mai had gathered for prayer together before the work of the day began when a faint unusual hum in the distance drew steadily nearer, and she recognised it as the sound of aeroplanes. An ominous sense of impending calamity deepened as the roar increased, and she found herself praying aloud, "Lord, protect us, you are over and above those planes."

Then came the sounds of explosions and crashing

masonry as again and again the planes swooped down nearly touching the roofs of buildings as they released their bombs, until at last they swept away, droning off into the distance, leaving Yangcheng a shambles.

Gladys emerged from the rubble and broken furniture that had turned the tidy room into a rubbish heap, and looked round. The others were scrambling slowly to their feet too, and they stood and looked at each other, faces bruised and blackened, thankful to be alive. The whole pattern of life had changed in that one terrifying hour, but life and limb had been preserved.

"My room was lop-sided and everything smashed in it. No way of getting out, only climbing through a hole in the wall, and oh, the mess! No roof left, piles of debris. But I soon realised if we had been hit so had others," so burrowing for her little first-aid box under the rubbish, she went out into the street, Ru Mai following.

The sight that met her eyes would have been too much for her had it not been for an indefinable calm that possessed her. The people of Yangcheng, completely unaccustomed to the sound of aeroplanes, had emerged with excited interest from their homes to look at the two silver birds flying above them. When the bombs fell they were defenceless. They lay now, many of them dead, others wounded, and those who were unhurt panic-stricken and bewildered. They had never known anything like this before, and those who were not stunned by the shock of it were distraught.

If Gladys had never actually been in a zeppelin raid over London in the First World War, at least she knew what had happened in them, and although this onslaught was much more fierce and concentrated she was not in any doubt as to what had taken place. The Japanese had bombed Yangcheng, and they might do it again. She moved straight into the situation as she found it, and wherever she went she brought a semblance of order and reassurance into the confusion, for she seemed to know what to do. Where she saw bodies trapped under masonry she started to get them out, snapping out sharp orders to the dazed onlookers.

"Here you! Come and get this man out. Careful, careful! Move that stone first. . . . Hot water! I want hot water! Quick woman, haven't you got any hot water in your kitchen? Ru Mai, you can bathe that child's leg and get the dirt out! Oh!" There was a body, lifeless, and after a moment's pause she said, "Cover it over. There's nothing we can do for him now. We must help those who are still alive."

She moved slowly along the streets that day, her face set, Chinese gown dirty and smeared with blood, yet with an authority which even the local soldiers recognised as she rapped out commands which they instantly obeyed. She seemed the one person who knew what to do, and they responded with relief that someone was in control. Not for hours did a tear come to her eyes, and then what brought it was the sight of an old man hugging a little girl of about three years old. He brought the child to her, begging her to save her, but one look, and Gladys saw that she was dead. She shook her head sadly, and as others crowded round for help the old man went wailing away, still hugging the precious little body. Gladys felt something come up in her own throat, a sob forcing its way out at last.

It was a day long to be remembered, for when eventually she reached the *Yamen* she was so dirty and dishevelled, and in tears by this time, that they did not recognise her at first. Not so did she usually enter the Mandarin's official residence! But when a basin of hot water was brought for her to wash, she was told comfortingly,

"Never mind, Teacher, we have caught the spy who gave warning to the planes."

She merely nodded. The word "spy" meant nothing to her then. Her mind was filled with the devastation and tragedy she had seen, and when she had pulled herself together she went back into the streets of the city to help whom she might. Then it was that she heard the name of the "spy" who had been arrested. It was one of the men she knew, a member of her little Christian community.

Back to the *Yamen* she sped, oblivious now to the sights and sounds around her. He couldn't have done this thing! She knew he couldn't! She must save him! She pleaded to be allowed to see him, to find out the truth, the explanation. But it was in vain. "You go and find a Chinese gentleman to stand with you," she was told, and she went off, her head in a whirl, her heart like a tight, tense knot, to try and find someone to go with her to speak for the prisoner. She could find no-one. Everyone was afraid, and anyhow, what did they really know about the man? What did she herself really know about him?

In the end she crept back to her own shattered home, shook the glass and bricks and rubbish off her bed and lay down, weeping and praying for strength. Ru Mai came to her, made her eat some food, and then together the two women lay on the bed, shivering, and somehow she slept.

"I rose early next morning," she wrote home later, "and, as I know China, I set off, but again I could find no

57

one to come with me, and I started for the *Yamen* with leaden feet, when I heard shouting and yelling. I put my fingers in my ears and ran, but oh, my darlings, I was too late; his poor body lay headless and bleeding at my feet. It seemed as if my heart would break. Oh China, poor China! Pray, dears, for his dear mother and his sweet little wife and little ones and another one soon to come; how could I tell them?

"I started back home, to find a load of wounded from the previous day's awful raids waiting for my help, so set to work with a sore and heavy heart, not daring to tell anyone, for to be even thought a spy is serious. Even though he was innocent, I had no proof but my knowledge of him as a Christian co-worker. Oh God, how long? Keep me faithful and give me strength till He comes!"

The city was in a panic, for during the night Chinese soldiers had entered, evidence that they were in the fighting zone now. People were pouring out of the gates, possessions piled high on their carts and their wheelbarrows, fleeing to the country. A group of Christian men came into the city to urge her to leave. "You must get out," they said. "You must all get out." They did not say why. They did not so much as give voice to the rumour that the Japanese were advancing. One did not say these things openly – not yet. But Gladys understood.

"All right," she said. "I'll do what you say. But I can't be bothered to pack my things. I must go first and see those people who were hit," and off she went, to do what she could for those whom she knew to be lying wounded in their homes. When she got back her things had been packed and taken off, the children with them, and only

Ru Mai and two of the men remained, to escort her to the little village of Peh Chia Chuang.

As she looked round on her ruined home, the place where she had built her hopes, had her dreams, held her meetings, the place that had become more dear to her than anywhere else on earth, she wept weakly. This was the hardest moment for her, she admitted later, leaving it, as she thought, for ever. Rather solemnly she knelt amidst the ruins, bowing before her God. When she rose to her feet again, she was quite calm.

For the next six days she went into the city each morning, to tend the wounded until the sound of the guns came so near the city that the order was given that it must be evacuated. Then she set up a "hospital" for wounded soldiers in a stable in the village, and those who had nowhere else to go, went there.

But there was something else on her mind beside the wounded. The little family of the executed "spy" was suspect, and Gladys *must* do something.

She hid them for three days then decided to take them to a safer place and finally after four days hiding and walking reached Tsechow with them.

The Japanese had gained control of Tsechow, which had put up little resistance, and on that first invasion they were behaving reasonably well. Gladys marched through the streets to the Mission compound, and remained there until the Japanese retreated, for it was filled with refugees and there was plenty to be done. As soon as the way was clear, however, she was back again in Yangcheng, and from there set off to see how the little group of Christians in Chinsui had fared. It was two days' journey away, in a very scattered mountain district, and when she arrived in a nearby village she had a great reception. News that Ai Weh Teh had come reached the Chinese general in Chinsui City and he sent an escort with a horse for her, so she rode in in great style. She was, as she expressed it in a letter to Evelyn, enjoying herself A.1. when a man came breathlessly with a message from David Davies. The Japanese were advancing again and he urged her to come back to Tsechow immediately.

So again she was on the run. Too late to get to Tsechow she found refuge in a Christian home in a village, and remained there for two months, sometimes not daring to go outside the front door, for it was right in the line of attack, and the guns were roaring and bullets whizzing along the streets. When the wave of fighting ebbed she made her way to Yangcheng again, through burnt out villages where the dead lay still unburied, back to the city itself, up the street that led to her compound, and into the shattered shell of a house that was her home.

It was still her home, and she intended to remain there. God had brought her to Yangcheng, of that she was sure, and the people of Yangcheng were her people. She would die with them, but she would never desert them. She clambered over the rubble into her room and looked round. Everything of value had been taken to Peh Chia Chuang and what had been left after that had been looted. But on one of the walls, where she had hung it months before, was a little motto card for the year 1938, clean and unharmed, and on it was the explanation of why she, a London parlourmaid who had never passed an examination in her life, was there. She read the words again, as she had read them many times before,

"God hath chosen the weak things."

And underneath that announcement of the selection of Omnipotence was what she claimed as her own response,

"I can do all things through Christ who strengtheneth me."

That was it. That was why she could speak these dialects of the Shansi mountains like a native now, why she could bring order out of chaos to distracted people, and tackle the nursing of wounded men. It was her first experience of such work, but "as we go on, so does God", and the success of her amateur efforts was proof of it. "It's not me, it's my God!" she protested when the wide-eyed peasants marvelled at how much she knew.

Letters from Yangcheng to London got through slowly and uncertainly in those days, but one reached the Aylward home in Edmonton containing a paragraph which was immortalized as the little parlourmaid became an almost legendary figure. She wrote in her usual artless style, about the things she was doing, the sort of food she was eating, about Ninepence, who had referred to her as a nice old lady – "so now you know what I am in the eyes of a child of eight." Then she continued more sombrely,

"Life is pitiful, death so familiar, suffering and pain so common, yet I would not be anywhere else. Do not wish me out of this or in any way seek to get me out, for I will not be got out while this trial is on. These are my people, God has given them to me, and I will live or die with them for Him and His glory."

# CHAPTER SEVEN

# David's Dilemma

David Davies had several things weighing on his mind as he trudged northwards from Kaifeng over the mountains back to Tsechow at the turn of the year 1939–40. In the first place, he had not got his passport. It had been taken from him by the Japanese at Kaifeng. His permit did not allow him to go any further, so the only way to get back was to leave the passport with them and give them the slip, which he did by keeping clear of the main roads and railways. The dykes of the Yellow River had been opened in an effort to hold back the advancing Japanese armies, and off the beaten track the going was hard, travelling across vast stretches of flooded territory where deserted villages crumbled into the water. Sometimes there was no road at all, only a ramshackle ferry boat or a ricketty bridge of planks hastily contrived by such peasants as still clung tenaciously to what was left of their farms and their homes.

At any rate Tsechow wouldn't be flooded, he consoled himself as he waded where he could not walk. Then he sighed. It might not be flooded by water, but it would be flooded by refugees, fleeing the flood and fleeing the famine, like human ants scattering in all directions as disaster on disaster struck their lives. The scorched earth policy might hamper the Japanese but it was a calamity of the first order for those whose homes were on the earth that was scorched. . . . He could see little but more sorrow, more suffering, more terror for the peasants of Shansi in the months ahead. The Japanese hold on the main lines of communication was strengthening, and the Chinese were finding it harder and harder to break those lines in sporadic attacks from their village hide-outs.

What was even worse – the seeds of civil war were already being sown. Skilfully the Chinese communists from their stronghold in Yenan were deploying their dedicated forces among the lawless and discontented. The gentlemanly highwaymen of the past were easily per-suaded to become the "Red Bandits" of the present. There was a mysterious guerrilla army on the field now with supplies of smuggled opium passing through their hands and ways of extracting money that made people cold and silent with fear.

Oh for the old times when Tsechow and Yangcheng lived under the easy-going rule of their magistrates and their local militia! It was bad enough when a battalion of Nationalist soldiers entered, expecting free billets and food. It was much worse when the Japanese clattered in after their thunderous bombardments, passions aflame for rape and revenge. But worst of all was the fear of the "Red Bandit" guerrillas.

Altogether, David Davies realised that he was engaged on a risky business, returning to that Mission compound in Tsechow, where over one hundred schoolchildren and a score of women had taken refuge from the varying perils that lurked in the No-Man's-Land of the fighting zone. So far it had been more or less inviolate as the property of an English Mission, Chinese and Japanese alike refraining from giving offence to a neutral power. Whether England would remain a neutral power was open to question, now that war had broken out in Europe. Already there were ominous signs that the Japanese sympathies were with the Nazis. One thing was off his mind, at any rate! His wife and children were safely settled at the famous seaside resort at Chefoo, with Murray in the China Inland Mission school there and American warships ready to whisk them off to safety in the event of trouble.

So thought David, ploughing on, in merciful ignorance of all that lay ahead – including the Japanese attack on Pearl Harbour. At any rate his own family, though on his heart, were not on his mind, and he was thankful. He had plenty of other matters to weigh on him, and amongst them was Gladys.

He was fond of Gladys, although he did not always approve of her actions. She had been a good friend to Jean and himself. How their hearts had warmed at the welcome she prepared for them when they first arrived, and how young Murray had gone to put his little hand in hers, right from the start! How touched they had been when she returned from a holiday at Tientsin bringing an enormous toy boat for him which must have cost far more than she could afford! She had always been ready to come to Tsechow at a moment's notice to keep Jean company while he was away somewhere, or to look after the children when Jean had to go to hospital. When there had been wounded men to tend after a wave of fighting she had come alongside with all the calm efficiency of a trained nurse, gritting her teeth as she helped him saw off shattered, hanging limbs.

"Gladys is trumps," he and Jean agreed, "ask her to do anything, and she'll do it."

The difficulty was, that she was the same with all her friends, as David discovered on his return to Tsechow. To his dismay and indignation he learned that while she had been there in charge she had allowed some Nationalist officers to come onto the compound to hold a feast.

"But Gladys, you know perfectly well I won't allow men on the compound!" Had she forgotten that the first time the Japs ever came to Tsechow they had found some able-bodied men on the compound, and lined them all up and shot them dead? Hadn't that been the bitter lesson that made him, David, realise he would never be able to protect men, and that his only hope of protecting women and children against invading armies was to have a compound where no men were suspected of lurking? What would happen if the Japanese returned and learned that Nationalist soldiers had been carousing there? How to convince them that at the Christian Mission strict neutrality was observed?

Silence. It was to Gladys' credit that when she had nothing to say she did not try to say it.

Furthermore, so David had heard, the Nationalist officers had drunk wine at their feast. David was a Welshman, and with the fluency of his race demanded to know what sort of reputation the Christian Mission would get with wine flowing with who knows what results! What sort of example was that to the young?

"How was I to know they'd have wine?" retorted Gladys.

How indeed? David realised that what could have been merely a parrying question with most people was, in her case, a genuine one. She was really too naïve for words was Gladys, taking everyone at their face-value! It would not have occurred to her that the courteous, charming young man who approached her about that little matter of the feast would be anything else but courteous and charming throughout, conducting themselves with quiet decorum and washing down their food with weak tea. For all her courage and her compassion, her faith and her dedication, when it came to matters that required sound judgment, Gladys was – well to put it politely, she was unwise. She admitted it herself sometimes, though the word she used was "silly"! Just silly! Well, if that was what she said about herself, David would not argue with her. Not for a moment would he argue as to whether silly was the right word! He sighed impatiently, shrugged his shoulders and then gave a little grin. It was no use being angry with her. She couldn't help it. She was made that way!

Nevertheless, the incident served to increase one of the weights on David's mind. Gladys was a member of the tiny Mission of which he and Jean were now the only other two left in China, and he felt responsible for her. If the Japanese attitude towards Britishers hardened, and he had to cut and run for it, what would happen to her? He thought almost with envy of those other men missionaries he knew who, armed with the indisputable authority "the Mission says . . ." were chasing around the province rounding up women fellow workers and bringing them in to the central stations, ready for a quick get-away if necessity arose.

It wouldn't be any use trying that on Gladys.

In the first place, he could not quote that conveniently

impersonal body "the Mission", because as they both knew, he *was* the Mission.

In the second place, she would have resigned on the spot if he threatened to move her from Yangcheng to a place of safety. She was prepared to die for Yangcheng, but not to desert it. All this David knew, so he wisely did not broach the subject at all. Nor did he give voice to his deepest fear for her. He was not so much afraid that if she fell into Japanese hands she would be beaten up, or even killed. She was prepared for that, just as he was. No, he was afraid of something else. Tsechow had been occupied more often, and for longer periods, than Yangcheng, and he knew what had happened to some of the women the Japanese soldiers had taken off to their barracks. . . .

He did not want that to happen to Gladys.

It was bad enough to know it was happening to little Chinese teenagers, squealing and sobbing in their agony of pain and shame. It would be worse to know it was happening to a fellow countrywoman and a fellow worker, and David wished with all his heart that he could persuade Gladys to get out of the danger zone. So what with anxiety provoking earnest desire, and desire turning to ardent prayer, an idea had formed in his mind which was to prove the solution of several problems.

Meanwhile Gladys was becoming more and more deeply involved with the Chinese Nationalists. Most of the peasants of the mountains were thankful if they could keep clear of soldiers, no matter which of the three fighting forces they represented. All they wanted was to be allowed to farm their land, go to market with their wares, live their lives as their fathers had lived, and die as their fathers had died. A few were dedicated to their country

and ready to die for it. Some saw the chance of a little
personal gain from helping this side or that side, which
they did at the risk of their lives, departing as speedily as
they could into the anonymous countryside when there
was a changeover.

At every changeover there were bound to be a few who
came under suspicion and were executed as "spies", and
as far as Gladys was concerned by the time 1940 dawned
a spy she was. When she went off, basket over her arm, to
visit remote villages where Christians were living, she
came back and gave information about the movement of
Japanese troops she saw in the neighbourhood. She had
no compunction about doing this – wasn't she a Chinese
citizen now, and weren't the Japanese invading her
country?

She was becoming a well-known figure in that turbu-
lent countryside. She helped train country women to do
Red Cross work, she was on terms of personal friendship
with the Nationalist General in the district and there was
a young Colonel Lin in the Intelligence Service with
whom she held conversations in David's office of a longer
duration than was usual for the energetic Ai Weh Teh.
Linnan she called him, and she told him all she knew.

All over the province of Shansi missionaries from
Britain were objects of suspicion to the Japanese, and
Ai Weh Teh was not the only one who eventually had a
price on her head. It is doubtful whether any of them had
given the invading Japanese greater cause to put it there!

One day, when the Davies's were away and Gladys was
in charge of Tsechow and Yangcheng, a young American
press correspondent, with the adventurous courage of his
kind, turned up. Theodore White was his name, and he

was gathering material about the conditions in war-torn China for the publication to which he contributed.

Gladys supplied him with it. In bald, vivid language she depicted the things she had seen and heard, running out every now and then to answer some call, issue some instruction, or listen for enemy planes. The young man was amazed. He had met plenty of missionaries on his travels, for missionaries were about the only westerners to be found in those rugged regions, but this one was exceptional. How she could talk, how graphically and intimately she could describe the chaos and the suffering! He stayed on an extra day to take in all he could, and then went on to the city where he was to stay with members of the Scandinavian Alliance.* When he arrived he could talk of nothing else but that little stick of an Englishwoman with her dark hair dragged back in a bun who was living alone there right on the firing line who knew everything that was going on and was evidently determined to stick it out whatever happened.

It was as well for the peace of mind of all concerned that they did not know the article he wrote for *Time* Magazine would be produced as further evidence against the prisoner when David Davies stood before a tribunal of Japanese officers, accused of being a spy....

\* \* \*

"It's these youngsters I'm worried about," said David to Gladys. She nodded. One hundred and more schoolboys and girls were apparently housed on the Tsechow compound now. So far they had escaped personal harm, but the Japanese always made a strong attack in the

* Now known as The Evangelical Alliance Mission of the U.S.A.

Spring, and it was likely to be an even stronger one this year. If they came and stayed, those youngsters would be "recruited" for Japanese purposes. If they came and did not stay, it was more than likely that it would be the Communist guerrillas, the "Red Bandits" who would take their place – and the youngsters would be "recruited" for Communist purposes.

"We must get them out. We must get them to the western provinces." David and Gladys were agreed it must be so.

It was happening all over China, that trek inland to the cities of the west – Sian, Chengtu, Chungking. Among the millions of distracted refugees were hundreds of groups of schoolchildren and college students, travelling with teachers to set up school and college again in more primitive but more peaceful surroundings. Sitting there in David's office in Tsechow, it was agreed that those youngsters must be got across the mountains, across the Yellow River to Sian, capital of Shansi, one-time capital of the Chinese Empire, to which place, it seemed, the Japanese could not possibly reach.

"Someone will have to go with them," said David.

"Yes," said Gladys.

"It can't be me," went on David, "I've been away too long already. Didn't expect that hold up in Kaifeng – then having to come the slow way because of having no pass. Besides, if for some reason I couldn't get back I'd be cut off from Jean and the children. . . ."

Gladys agreed it could not be David who took the children to Sian. She pursed her lips, reckoned it would not take anyone more than a month to escort them there and then get back – probably less.

"Please God, you won't get back!" thought David fervently. But he didn't say so. He just said they'd have to let the parents of the children know what was being planned, and find out if they wanted them to go. As the Japanese offensive was already beginning, decisions were made swiftly. One batch of about one hundred children was dispatched almost immediately to Sian, and rather to David's dismay it was a local man, not Gladys, who agreed to be in charge of that party. But news of what was happening had got around and more parents arrived with their children, begging that they might be taken too –

"He's fifteen already – he'll be conscripted...."

"Please take her – how can we protect a girl of thirteen?"

Some children were just quietly brought to the compound and left there. The same thing was happening in Yangcheng. And the Japanese offensive was speeding up. The main routes were already closing, and another batch of children must be got to Sian.

David and Gladys looked into each other's eyes, thoughtfully. There was no need to discuss who should escort the party, to David's relief. There was nothing more they could do to help each other, either. They were both under Authority, and they knew it.

*"I say to this man, Go, and he goeth; and to another, Come, and he cometh; and to my servant. Do this, and he doeth it."*

The parting of the ways had come, and as things worked out they did not meet again for ten years. David remained in Tsechow to be arrested by the Japanese, endure months of torture and years of imprisonment, one of the many unrecorded heroes of World War Two.

71

Gladys set off on the epic trek with the children over the mountains to Free China that was to capture the imagination of millions of people and bring her to fame.

To neither did the outcome of their decision really matter. All that mattered was that they were obeying orders to the best of their ability.

And since the future, as usual, was completely veiled, and the present was just like it had been for the years they had been fellow workers, they discussed things quite prosaically, prayed that God would continue to guide and help them, and left it at that. The compound was swarming with refugees, the Japanese were advancing and the sooner the children could be got away to Yangcheng the better. The trek to Sian must start from there.

CHAPTER EIGHT

# Trek with the Children

If Gladys Aylward had not got away with those children when she did, she would probably never have been heard of again. The Japanese were in control of the main routes, the Chinese Nationalists were retreating, and in the hamlets and villages of the vast mountainous area the "Red Bandits" were pillaging and harrying. She had a price on her head by this time. The Japanese were prepared to pay one hundred dollars for information leading to her capture.

One hundred dollars was a lot of money there West of the Mountains and there would be plenty of people ready to betray her to obtain it, as she very well knew. There would be no-one to ask any awkward questions, either. She was no longer a British citizen, about whom the British Government would institute official enquiries if she disappeared. She was just a naturalised Chinese woman now, and a poor one at that. When she stopped to think about it she was downright scared, until with lips pursed she reminded herself that God was with her, and that whatever happened He would never let her down.

Her mind was in a turmoil nevertheless, and she could not bring herself to leave until an urgent message from God Himself, as she firmly believed, convinced her that she must go. "Flee ye, flee ye into the mountains; dwell deeply in hidden places, because the King of Babylon has conceived a purpose against you," she read when she opened her Chinese Bible after a desperate prayer that she would be shown what to do. That verse settled it. God had spoken, and flee she must.

So one Spring morning in 1940 she set off with that heterogeneous company of children – some from the school at Tsechow, some from families around Yangcheng, others little waifs who had been left over from the pitiful treks of the refugees fleeing from the fighting and the floods and the famine. Every child had a bowl and chopsticks, a face towel and a little quilt for bedding. The teenage boys manfully shouldered further supplies. The local magistrate sent a couple of men with supplies of food swinging from their carrying poles, to accompany the party for the first two or three days. They surged out through the broken down gates of battered Yangcheng, the children at any rate merry enough, and Gladys never saw the city again.

Ninepence was in the company, of course, and Ru Mai's daughter, along with some other teenage girls. Gladys had a special plan for them. She and Ru Mai had seen an advertisement urging people to get their girls away from the Japanese to an organisation called "Good News", in a place called Fufeng in Shensi. After delivering the younger children to Madame Chiang's relief orphanage, therefore, they would take the teenage girls to Fufeng. Since "Good News" was the term used for the Gospel, Gladys jumped to the conclusion that it was a Christian Church affair. The conclusion proved to be very wrong indeed, and yet it had an important bearing on what happened later.

It was all fairly easy going the first day out, with plenty of food, and everyone in high spirits, and in familiar country. They all slept the first night in the shelter of a Buddhist temple. The next night, after trudging all day, they had to sleep out, huddling together at the foot of some rocks. They were moving out into unknown territory now, and the following day the two men left them to return to Yangcheng. All the food had been eaten, and from that time on they would have to fend for themselves.

There has never been any available record of that journey other than that which Gladys Aylward herself supplied. As far as can be ascertained, the astute Ru Mai was with her, but there is no evidence of any other adult being in the party. They straggled on, score upon score of refugee children trailing across that rugged, mountainous No Man's Land, a sharp-eyed, wiry little woman who still spoke her fluent Chinese with the hint of a Cockney accent overseeing the whole fantastic exodus. Sometimes they got to a small town and she went and begged food from the magistrate, sometimes villagers took pity on them, sometimes they had help from Chinese soldiers who were stationed in little bands here and there, the rearguard of the retreating army. They warned her the Japanese were advancing. She would have to hurry if she were to get her crowd of children across the Yellow River before the Japanese got there.

The children got weary. The rollicking enthusiasm of the first day or two gradually wore away, and the little ones were fretful, wanting to be carried, wanting to stop, wanting to go back home. Gladys cuffed them and pushed them and carried them and cheered them forward, calling out,

"Come now, let's sing! All together! Ready?" and they would pipe up,

"Count your blessings, name them one by one,
Count your blessings, see what God has done,
    Count your blessings,
    Name them one by one,
And it will surprise you what the Lord has done!"

On they went, the older boys going ahead to plot out the way, the teenage girls hobbling rather painfully, the more adventurous children hiving off here and there, all of them getting more dishevelled, urged on by Gladys,

"Hi, what are you doing, you kids? Stop larking about there, you two boys, and move up to the front. Do you hear me? Up to the front where I can see you ...

"Hello, girlie, are your feet hurting? Here, I'll carry that basket for you for a little while ... What's that, sonny? Tired? We'll soon be at the Yellow River. Look, I'll give you a pick-a-back – how about that? Up you get!

"Oh dear, you're tired too, Little Sister? I can't give you both a pick-a-back at once. Liang! Liang!" calling to one of the older boys, "There's a little girl who needs carrying for a while – can you take her? Good! On we go now, let's sing again,

"The Lord's my shepherd, I'll not want ..."

At last after days of struggling along, they got to the Yellow River. There it was, so wide, so deep, and the opposite bank so far away. There was not the sign of a boat to take them across, and the little town where they had expected to get food and shelter was deserted. Only a few soldiers were there, who provided them with some thin porridge, and after they had swallowed it hungrily they went back to the bank of the river, waiting for a ferry to take them across.

But no ferry came. The ferry was closed. Rumour had it that the short, sturdy little men from Japan, well-trained, well-equipped, fierce and dedicated were marching towards the river, and should they find boats handy to carry them across? No indeed! All the boats were on the other side, and there they would stay.

Many and many a time had Gladys told the story of how the children of Israel escaped out of Egypt and came to the banks of the Red Sea, the Egyptians in hot pursuit. Many and many a time had she related how that vast company stood helplessly looking at the expanse of water in front of them, the enemy coming up behind, and no way of escape. Many and many a time had she depicted the scene with such dramatic imagination that she might have been there herself – but she was experiencing reality now.

She looked round the dusty bank, where the children were sitting or sprawling, some playing, some whimpering a little, all hungry, all grubby. And all her responsibility. Her responsibility – the thought weighed on her, and she felt resentful. Why must she look after all those kids? If it were not for them she could have been here days before, safely over that river, safe from the advancing Japanese.

That second night by the Yellow River was the worst Gladys had ever known. They had waited all day for a boat to appear, but the river had remained empty, flow-ing, flowing, flowing down towards the south.

"When are we going to cross the river?" the children had asked, and she could not answer them. The older teenagers had glanced at her from time to time, but said nothing. They knew what the younger ones did not realise. They were stranded there, cut off, too late for the ferries that had taken over the other parties of refugees. They had arrived too late. They could not go on, they could not go back, and the Japanese were coming.

Gladys lay all that night trying not to think about what happened to women when the Japanese took them. ...

The next morning was just like the other two. There was no sign of life on the river. But that morning one of the teenage girls came and asked Gladys a question. If God, in the time of Moses, had opened the Red Sea to let the children of Israel through, why didn't he open the Yellow River to let them, the refugee children from West of the Mountains, go through also?

Gladys was irritated by the question. That was in the time of Moses, she retorted tartly, and she was not Moses!

"You are not Moses, but God is still God," replied the girl. "Isn't He?"

Yes. Of course. God is still God.

Gladys, grim-faced, stared unseeing before her. Yes. God is still God. That's it. That's our only hope – God.

It's over to you now, God. I'm finished. Oh God, do something for us now. Don't let us down. Help us, God. Get us to the other side of the river. Oh Lord, get us over the river....

After they had prayed Gladys lay down, exhausted.

78

She did not know how long she had been there when the excited cries of the children, tugging at her jacket, roused her. A tall young officer of the Chinese Nationalists was approaching. She had not seen him before. He asked her a few questions, and then went to the edge of the water and whistled.

"I'll get a boat for you," he said. "You must get over as soon as possible."

Away on the other side of the river a boat drew out from a little creek and was rowed steadily across the waters. The children lined up, chattering eagerly, and batch after batch were rowed over.

The Yellow River didn't open for them, but they got to the other side just the same. She wasn't Moses, and the Yellow River wasn't the Red Sea, Gladys reflected – but God was still God.

*       *       *

She felt safer once they were all across. The villages weren't so deserted, there were more people about, and the river flowed between them and the enemy. But Sian was still a long, long way.

They walked, then they boarded a refugee train, crowded with people and bundles, and with some people clinging on outside. Then they walked again, over another mountain range. Then they all clambered onto a coal train, crouching on the laden trucks that rumbled slowly through the night, close to where the Japanese might snipe at it. They were covered with coal dust when they slithered off the train. She tried to make the kids wash their faces, but she was getting too tired to bother much. Just as long as they had something to eat, and kept going, she thought. There were refugee centres along the way, so that made it easier. She was very tired. She'd be glad when they got to Sian.

But when at last they got there, she could not get in. The great walled city was already full of refugees – men, women, children, old grannies, with their boxes and their bundles and their baskets, bewildered, looking for lodgings, the streets were swarming with them. The gates were closed to refugees, and they must go somewhere else.

Gladys wept weakly. She was seriously ill by this time, though she did not know it. Something was burning within her, urging her on. Where to go now? Sian had been the promised land, Sian was where the children were to find their refuge, and now Sian was closed. There was no other plan in her mind except – what was that place where the teenage girls were to go? Fufeng. Fufeng. They would go to Fufeng.

All the trains were carrying refugees, free of charge, and they got on a train to Fufeng, swept along with the human tide. It was when they reached Fufeng that she collapsed, like a gallant little sparrow battered by the gales that falls to the ground at last.

She might have fallen anywhere along the way she had come, over those desolate mountains, on the banks of the Yellow River, on the crowded trains, in the towns and villages through which they had passed, or just by the side of a country track. In all those places she was a complete stranger, a tiny woman looking like one of the hundreds of thousands of Chinese women among whom she had mingled on that incredible journey. Only the cast of her features, sharp and narrow compared with their broad, flat faces revealed that she was not Chinese. She had no identification papers. No one was on the look-out for her. The only westerner who even knew she was making for Sian was David Davies, and by this time he was a captive of the Japanese.

In Fufeng also she was a stranger. The "Good News" organisation for the teenage girls proved to be a sort of second-hand bureau for supplying healthy young females to families in the north-west, where women were in short supply. It was housed in a Buddhist temple. When she discovered the truth about it, months later, she was very angry, but she was at the point of delirium now, and conscious of nothing but a feverish urge to get out and preach. That was what she had come to China to do, to preach the Gospel! With feverish zeal she set out to do it. And while doing it she collapsed.

Now it so happened that in Fufeng there was a little Christian church. In that vast, thickly populated area round Sian there were scores of towns and hundreds of villages where there was no such thing, but in Fufeng there was. It was only a small affair, an obscure little compound to which missionaries went on a visit from time to time, though none were resident there. However, the handful of people in the town of Fufeng who were connected with it, in a dilemma with this wild but zealous woman, now unconscious, on their hands, knew where to take her. They did not know who she was, but they knew she was a Christian and they saw she was a westerner, so without hesitation they took her to the nearest missionary, an American in a city called Hsing Ping, some distance away.

He did not know who she was either, but that did not matter. Away there on the Sian plain Protestant missionaries were few and far between. They were all strangers in a strange land, they had come to it from vastly different backgrounds, but they had all come for the same purpose. God had called them. Most of them were quite sure about that. Irrespective of mission, nation or denomination they were bound together by their discipleship to Jesus Christ. They could be relied upon to help when called on, without explanation or apology, so the American missionary immediately took Gladys in, and the alert was sounded.

"Unknown British woman seriously ill doctor please come Gustafsen" he wired to the Baptist Missionary Society in Sian, then sent a message to an American nurse on another mission station to come at once. Dr. Handley Stockley beat the nurse to it. Sian and Hsing Ping were connected by the one and only railway line in that part of China, so he caught the next train, complete with blood film slides, medicines, needles, syringes, distilled water and intravenous saline of glucose.

Gladys was delirious, with a temperature of 105, and reacted violently against the doctor, who she was convinced was a Japanese officer up to no good. He managed to make some blood films and sent them off post haste to Sian for a report, which arrived the next day, confirming his fears that the patient had relapsing fever.

Gladys, of course, was unconscious of all this. Most of the time she was far away. She was back in World War 1, in the little terrace house in Edmonton, singing for all her worth the rattling songs that kept up the spirits of the boys in the Flanders trenches, the long way to Tipperary getting mixed up with dear old Blighty, and Mademoiselle from Armentiers popping in and out.

Then, suddenly, she was in the villages around Yang-cheng, talking, talking, talking to the peasants there about the Living God Who had sent his Son to save them from death and the devil....

No! She was with Queenie in the gallery of a theatre, peering down eagerly at the graceful couple spotlighted on the stage, humming as they crooned ...

She was screaming, yelling to the children in Tsechow, "Quick! Get under cover! The planes are coming!" Then she was talking to Mum and Vi, confiding an amusing incident involving her mistress, mimicking her....

She prayed ... In the middle of it she shouted to the gatekeeper in Yangcheng to bring her mule. She started to sing a hymn.

The doctor kept careful watch over her, checking her temperature, trying to quieten her, listening, trying to discover who she was. She was worn out with fatigue and malnutrition, it was a marvel she was still alive. The nurse had arrived by this time, and after he had given Gladys an injection he said,

"The fever will fall now. Her temperature will go below normal, and she'll perspire profusely. She'll be very weak after that. But I think you'll be all right with her now. Don't hesitate to let me know if you are worried...." and he returned to Sian.

He was back again five days later, in response to an anxious message from the nurse. The patient's temperature had fallen, then shot back to 105, and she was delirious again. As he was examining her he saw that a typhus fever rash was breaking out. She had also developed pneumonia.

There was no specific treatment for typhus fever in

those days, but Gustafsen, who had just returned from his leave in the U.S.A., had brought back with him some new drugs – Sulphapyridine, Sulphur 693. Any use to you? he asked the doctor. From the doctor's point of view they were providential, for he knew they were potent especially against pneumonia, and where else could he have laid hands on them, there in the middle of war-torn China? They were invaluable, and if Gustafsen could spare them. . . .

"Take them!" said Gustafsen. They were one more link in the long chain that drew her back from death.

"We must get her to hospital as soon as we possibly can," said the doctor. "Everything depends on careful, constant nursing now, day and night. And I want to keep an eye on her. . . ."

He returned to Sian, interviewing the official in charge of the railway line to ask for a special van to be attached to the evening train from Hsing Ping (they both belonged to the Rotary Club, and that made it easier to ask a favour) and hurried back to the hospital to make arrangements for receiving the mysterious, shrivelled little slip of a woman who raved in an uncouth Chinese dialect, interspersed with Cockney English.

There had been some alarming air-raids over Sian, so the hospital had been housed in a boys' school in the suburbs, and accommodation was limited. One of the lady doctors vacated her bedroom for her unknown fellow countrywoman. Gradually the fever abated, and after many days they learned her name at last. Gladys Aylward. Her family lived at 67 Cheddington Road, Edmonton. Mum would be worried. Yes, please, if someone would write to her. . . .

One Sunday, about ten days after Gladys' temperature had returned to normal, the air raid alarm which had been silent for several weeks sounded again. The missionary doctors and nurses on the hospital compound were in the habit of going to an English service held in Sian city every Sunday evening, and decided that, air raid or no air raid, they weren't going to be done out of it, and set off as usual. Dr. Stockley, however, remained behind. He was not sure how the sound of bombs exploding would react on his patient, whose recovery so far was something in the nature of a miracle.

It was as well that he did. When the roar of the planes was heard, and the bombs started exploding in the city, he witnessed the severest case of delayed shock he had ever seen. Gladys' thin little body twitched and trembled to such an extent that the bedstead on which she was lying shook and rattled, and he knew she must not go through that again.

"The planes will come again the same time tomorrow and the day after," he said. Three days bombing in succession was the usual pattern. "Must get her away somewhere before tomorrow evening!"

But get her where? That was the unsolved question until the arrival of a dog with an ingrowing toenail – or, to be strictly accurate, an ingrowing claw – led to the solution.

The dog's name was Alfie, and his master was Postal Director Smith. Postal Director Smith had moved all the G.H.Q. staff out of Sian on account of the heavy bombing, and all were now fairly comfortably accommodated in the Great Goose Pagoda, some six miles from the city. There it had become apparent that Alfie had something wrong with one of his paws. There being no veterinary surgeon to whom Postal Director Smith could entrust his pet, he brought him to the Baptist Mission hospital instead. After all, the Baptists were British as well as he, and the British are a nation of dog-lovers!

It was while Dr. Stockley was attending to Alfie's in-growing claw that the problem of where to get Gladys Aylward away from the bombing was discussed in the hearing of Postal Director Smith. "Bring her out to the Great Goose Pagoda," he said immediately. So to the Great Goose Pagoda they took her.

"Omnipotence," it has been truly said, "hath servants everywhere."

# CHAPTER NINE

# The Stub of a Sword

The Fishers were a popular couple. Their friends' faces relaxed into a grin when they were referred to, and they chuckled, "Dear old Hubert! Good thing he's got Mary to look after him!" Theirs was a comfortable sort of home to stay in, however busy they might be with their Bible classes and their prayer meetings, their visits to the out-stations and their preaching in the streets. Hubert's zeal had nothing of the fanatical about it, leaving plenty of room for humour, and Mary had sufficient of the Martha in her temperament to ensure that meals were tasty as well as nourishing, even when funds were low, as they often were in those war years.

Perhaps that is why the Baptist missionaries in Sian, looking round for a quiet home for Gladys, decided that Meihsien, with the Fishers, would be just the place for her.

As things turned out, they discovered that the Fishers had met her two or three years previously, when they were living West of the Mountains, Shansi. She had passed through their mission station to attend a conference, arriving unannounced one evening. She was accompanied by two Chinese women and a Chinese teenage lad, and the Fishers had scurried round to prepare a room for them, and give them a good meal before going to bed.

Next morning Gladys and her company had a very early prayer meeting. Prayer was mingled with singing, and the Fishers were awakened rather earlier than usual by the words of a hymn wafting across the courtyard at five a.m.

"When your fears rise mountain high...."

The quartette was singing fervently, and the sympathetic Fishers wondered what fears were alarming their guests. Judicious enquiries elicited the information that they had run out of money, so could not go on to the conference after all. The Fishers saw to it that the quartette got to the conference all right! The impression they gained of Gladys was "not that she was spongeing on us, but simply had not calculated well enough, and probably was not in the habit of doing so."

When they heard that she had brought some girls out from the No-Man's Land west of the mountains to Fufeng, been stricken down there suddenly with relapsing fever, and was now in Sian recovering from an illness that had threatened her life, they set off to see Dr. Stockley about her. They were actually at the railway station, waiting to board the train for Sian, when a tall westerner appeared before them, barring their way. They recognised him immediately.

"Well! Reuben Gustafsen! Glad to see you! What are you doing here?"

"Come to stop you going any farther," was the reply. "You'd better go back home. Gladys Aylward is there."

"Gladys Aylward in our home?"

"Yes. We'd brought her from the Great Goose Pagoda to Hsing Ping, intending to bring her to you in a few days' time, but there was an air raid warning, and she simply couldn't stand the sirens. Mildred Nelson and I have brought her here. We got into your place through a window when we found you weren't in," he cautioned, "Glad I got you in time. She's quite ill still – her mind's affected. Mildred's looking after her till you can take over."

So Gladys stayed with the Fishers, out of the sight and sound of the war, for six months. Her temperature was normal, but not her mind. There were times when she wandered around not knowing where she was or who she was. Occasionally she suffered from hallucinations. It was the result of the sustained high temperature, and Dr. Stockley had warned them that at times she would be deranged. She would need patient and careful handling.

She needed plenty of good food, too, the practical Mary Fisher decided, and set about giving it to her. Then it became evident that Gladys had dysentery, resulting in restrictions on diet that made things almost as hard for the nurse trying to tempt the patient to eat as for the patient who didn't really want to.

Gladys took that part of it cheerfully enough, and did not complain. She was never very interested in food. What she did want was someone to talk to, and as long as Mary Fisher would sit and listen to her stories about the old life in England or in Yangcheng, Gladys was happy and contented. When she was left alone for a while, however, Mary would come back and find her sitting and quietly weeping.

A year or two previously she had pasted into the fly leaf of her Chinese Bible a slip of paper on which were printed the words,

Many crowd the Saviour's Kingdom
    Few receive His Cross
Many seek His consolation
    Few will suffer loss
For the sake of the dear Master,
    Counting all but dross.

Many sit at Jesus' table
    Few will fast with Him
When the sorrow-cup of anguish
    Trembles to the brim....

Perhaps in those months when she was struggling back to health she tasted something of that anguish. There were times when she felt very near to death, and reading in the book of Psalms one day she came to the words, "I shall not die." She marked them and wrote in the margin beside them, "Sian, Meihsien, 1940." It was another of the messages that came to her direct from God, as she believed. But perhaps the verses that meant most to her then, and which she was to repeat innumerable times in the years to come, were those found in I Chronicles, chapter 22, which she translated from her Chinese Bible as, "Be strong and courageous. Do not be afraid, and do not wobble.... Is not your God with you?" She marked them in red, and in the margin above them wrote, "Meihsien, June 1940."

Although the periods of mental confusion recurred from time to time for several years, her physical strength gradually returned, and with it the old familiar urge to be out and about. Mary Fisher noticed with satisfaction that she was talking to the Chinese now, telling them her experiences, especially about how she had come to China, and the terrible things that had happened on that journey, and how God had delivered her out of them all.

The Chinese lapped it up. She started speaking at little meetings, always to a spellbound audience, and news about her spread abroad. After she had been with the Fishers for about six months it was decided that she was well enough to try living alone in one of the outstations.

And so she came back to Fufeng, where she had collapsed at the end of that trek over the mountains, and where the teenage girls were still housed in the temple. How glad she was to see them! She lived in the little three-roomed dirt-floored house on the church compound, Ru Mai joined her, and she reverted to the old familiar way of life. Chinese food, no set times for meals, toddling off, Bible under her arm and a roll of pictures to preach from, her days were spent wandering into courtyards where women sat stitching shoes, or spinning thread, ready to stop and talk – and listen!

She soon got tired, however, and had to lie often on the warm k'ang.* Without realizing it she missed those nourishing meals Mary Fisher had produced. It was only after she had been in Fufeng for several weeks that it dawned on her what the "Good News" organisation really was. It was no altruistic movement, but a profitable enterprise whereby a family with an unmarriageable dolt of a son could obtain a daughter-in-law, or a man with an ageing spouse a healthy young second wife all for the price of a mule.

* A k'ang is a raised brick platform used for sleeping built in houses in North China, which are kept heated during the winter.

Gladys was galvanised into indignant life. She had been deceived! Her girls were in danger of being sold off into a life of misery when she had believed they were being cared for by a Christian organisation. If those temple people thought they were going to dispose of her girls the way they liked, they were very much mistaken! She secretly organised a rescue operation, and the temple people awoke one morning to discover that half a dozen or so of the girls were missing. Ai Weh Teh had gone off with them, to Sian.

The temple people were furious. In the light of the customs of old China the organisation was acting very reasonably, finding suitable homes for refugee girls who had fled from the invader. Ai Weh Teh had voluntarily arranged for them to be taken in, housed and fed, and if they had more than earned their keep by the work they did while there, what more would be expected? Had they taken action against her she would probably have had a bad time of it, for her Chinese citizenship did nothing to improve her status with the authorities. That the temple people eventually decided to let the matter drop is one of the deliverances in her life only explained by her own assertion that God was with her.

Back in Sian, thin and still prone to periods of confusion when she wandered around the streets vacantly, the Baptist missionaries were worried about her. They consulted together and decided to approach the British Consul and ask if he could get her home to England. The war was raging in Europe, the coasts of China were all blockaded now, but there was still a way out over the Burma Road into India, and this penniless little English-woman, alone in China, was surely the responsibility of the British Government? It was then that they learned she was not an Englishwoman any more. She had taken out Chinese citizenship.

They looked at each other in dismay. What could they do for her now? She had been delivered at their gates, so to speak, at the brink of death, they had seen her slowly brought back to life, their admiration had been stirred by that dogged, cheerful spirit of hers, their loyalty and affection quickened by her Cockney wit and her Cockney courage. "London can take it!" the Londoners were writing defiantly on their pavements as they emerged from their air-raid shelters after another Blitz. Gladys could take it too.

> "More than half-beaten, but fearless,
> Facing the storm and the night,
> Reeling and breathless, but fearless,
> Here in the lull of the fight.
> I who bow not but before Thee,
> God of the fighting clan,
> Lifting my fists I implore Thee,
> Give me the heart of a man!"

The stirring verses were stuck in the flyleaf of her Bible, and ended with the words, "But spare me the stub of a sword." If the Baptist missionaries had noticed those verses, they would have agreed that a stub was all she seemed to have left now, as far as physical and mental equipment went....

She would always be one of them in a way – and yet in a way she would never be. That almost ruthless independence of hers set her apart. She had strong convictions at which she arrived without other people's advice, and could never be one of a team. "Me – and God" was the way she always saw it, and no other person really came into it.

"Look here, Gladys," said the Baptist missionaries. "Stay here as long as you need to. Come along any time you like – there'll always be a bed for you. If there's anything we can do for you, just let us know."

"All right," said Gladys. All through her life it was like that. There were always people who said to her, "Come along any time you like – anything we can do to help you, let us know." She took them at their word, too, turning up from time to time, unannounced, with a simple "It's me!", rather like a child sure of a welcome, staying for a while, then disappearing again, back among the Chinese.

It was with the Chinese she lived there in Sian, in a tiny room that opened onto a little square courtyard where a few hens pecked about, belonging to the other refugees who had settled there. The courtyard was rented by two men, Christians, who had fled from the eastern provinces to Sian to escape the invading Japanese, and one of the rooms was turned into a chapel. Rough, backless benches, brightly coloured Scripture posters on the wall, a brick platform at one end provided all that was necessary, and this place, known as the Independent Church, became a centre to which refugees who were Christians found their way. They came with their bundles and their babies, some with a few hens tied together by the legs and carried upside down, bewildered, frightened. Gladys, who knew just what they felt like, hurried forward to meet them, found places for them to sleep, got the fire going to make some food. When it rained the courtyard was a quagmire, and her tiny room, with its old chest of drawers and table and a couple of chairs and a wooden bedstead ranged against the walls, often sheltered others beside herself.

It was the young people who specially drew out her sympathy, and as the schools in Sian were now bulging with refugee children, many of them got into the habit of going along to the courtyard where Ai Weh Teh lived. Her knowledge of English was an attraction, and, in fact, she earned some money by giving lessons to a few officials who wanted to learn the language. The schoolchildren listened enthralled to her stories of life at home, where her father was a post-master and her brother one of the guards at Buckingham Palace! She found it easier to promote Dad and Laurie in this way than to go into laborious explanations about the different standards of living in the country she came from, where postmen were not in the least like the ragged, illiterate runners from the *Yamen*, nor soldiers like the undisciplined little groups of militia who roamed over the mountains. How else could she convey to them that her father was always spruce and tidy, and knew how to read all sorts of books? How else bring the picture before their minds of Laurie stepping it out smartly to the music of the regimental band? Her vivid imagination ran away with her as well as her hearers at times, in those gay recitals that whirled them all away from the drabness and the poverty that surrounded them.

But as she was talking her quick eyes were noting when some child had a rent in his clothes that required a patch, or that indispensable item, a face towel, that had worn to a rag, and in her practical, businesslike way she rummaged through her own scanty possessions to find what was required. She talked to them about God, and how He had sent her to China, just as surely as He had sent Moses to Egypt to bring out the Children of Israel. He was the same God now as He was then, and she urged them to trust in Him.

All the time, refugees were coming into Sian as the Japanese advanced in the provinces south of the Yellow River. They came on the crowded trains, clinging to the doors and windows, sprawling on the roofs. They came on loaded merchandise lorries, bouncing about on top. They came on bicycles, handle bars and carriers laden with bundles. Every now and then, among the thousands of Chinese, travel-stained missionaries would straggle in, bringing with them what possessions they could, thankfully making their way to the hospitable compound of the Baptist Missionary Society or the Scandinavian Alliance Mission.

Jumble sales were the order of the day then, for they had to turn their possessions into cash if they were to proceed further west, and jumble sales were right in Gladys' line! She knew better than most what prices could be fetched for the garments and household linen and tea-pots and cutlery and old tin cans that were heaped in glorious confusion in the class room turned second-hand shop.

"You ought to get six dollars for that towel," she said, "and someone might be very proud of that teapot – might pay twenty dollars for it. Not easy to get anything for that cutlery – but this tin box! Why, it's got a lid! You'll sell that all right – ten dollars at least. I suppose you haven't got any empty kerosene tins? They're priceless!

96

The water carriers will pay any amount for them – so much lighter than their old wooden buckets. . . ."

She was helping at the sale one day when a refugee missionary from one of the provinces south of the river came up to her and said eagerly.

"I say, I've just heard that you're Gladys Aylward! I'm awfully glad to meet you. I read about your coming to China all alone in a little magazine some years ago, and I've been praying for you ever since. I didn't know you were here."

"Would you like to come and see where I live?" enquired Gladys. "We could go along when the sale's over, if you like." So they set off together, along the broad muddy streets until they turned into a side road, and then into the little square courtyard, over to one of the doors with a padlock on the outside, which Gladys unlocked.

"Here it is," she said, as she opened the door onto her tiny room. "I've got a widow woman and a baby staying here with me just now. They'll be back soon."

The other looked round silently. She had come from a very small mission station herself, where she and her fellow worker had been the only westerners in the whole area. They had lived very simply, in a little three-roomed Chinese house behind the big barn that had been converted into a chapel. From there they made their trips into the villages around, returning after a few days to drag out the big tin bath tub and thankfully wash themselves all over in the bucket full of hot water that had been heated by their serving woman on the kitchen fire. If they were smart enough they could get rid of most of the fleas by throwing all their clothes outside as they undressed, so that when they donned a fresh lot of clothes they were more or less free of them. Their little courtyard was very small, boasting only an acacia tree and a couple of rose bushes, but it was secluded, and their kitchen, smothered in smuts from the fire of coal dust, was at least their own.

But this was different. This was a communal compound, with a shed in the corner for a kitchen, open to the weather and used by all, and a latrine that was just a hole in the ground behind a wall. There was no privacy in that tiny room, for when the occupant was at home the door would be, of course, left open. Whoever heard of anyone going into their home and closing the door in the daytime? When Gladys wanted a bath she would have to do the best she could late at night, discreetly, in her face basin. The little room was meticulously tidy, with a few tiny photographs in tin frames on the chest of drawers, and an enormous thermos flask to be filled up once a day with boiling water, so that she could always have a drink of hot weak Chinese tea to wash down a meal composed of coarse bread and a little pickled vegetable.

"It's not easy to get a meal here," said Gladys. "I know a little restaurant not far away, where we can buy something." So they went along to an open fronted shop with a few rough benches and trestle tables, where coolies came in for their bowls of hot noodles, and there, as they ate, Gladys talked. She spoke almost as though she were in a trance, her dark eyes brooding, glowing.

"All those kids! A long line of them stretching right over the mountain. I couldn't think how I'd been so silly as to take the job on. I started crying once and all the kids saw me and started crying too. So there we were, howling as we went on, trailing along over the mountain. . . . Oh

God, why have you landed me with all these kids? I said.

"I was awfully ill, for months. They thought I was going to die. I guess I'd have been glad to, sometimes. Even after I was able to get around again, I was confused. Wandered around. Still do, sometimes. Sometimes one of the kids sees me, and brings me back!

"I was restless, too. Unsatisfied. There was a young man once." She was silent for a moment, brooding, and her companion waited, asking no questions, just listening.

"There was a young man once . . ." She did not say who he was. She did not say his name was Linnan. "I don't know what he must have thought," she said. So whatever it was, it had come to an end, thought her companion.

"It was a Chinese bishop who helped me," went on Gladys. "I told him how I was feeling – restless, unhappy. I was lonely – terribly lonely. It is lonely, you know, not belonging to any group. It's different for the other missionaries. They've all got their own missions. They all belong. It's lonely being one on your own. . . .

"That Chinese bishop helped me. He said, 'Gladys, it's marriage you're wanting. You can't go on like this. You'll either have to get married or – you'll have to trust the Lord to satisfy your desires in His own way. He knows you. He made you. He can satisfy your emotional needs – if you trust Him.'

"So that's it," said Gladys.

They looked at each other across the rough table, and nodded. There were some things they understood without speech. They were not Roman Catholic nuns, they had taken no vows, they led no cloistered existence, and yet,

*"He said unto them, all men cannot receive this saying*

*save they to whom it is given. . . . There be eunuchs which have made themselves eunuchs for the kingdom of heaven's sake. He that is able to receive it, let him receive it."*

*"Sing, O barren, thou that didst not bear; break forth into singing and cry aloud, thou that didst not travail with child: for more are the children of the desolate than the children of the married wife, saith the Lord . . . for thou shalt forget the shame of thy youth and shalt not remember the reproach of thy widowhood any more. . . . For thy Maker is thy husband; the Lord of hosts is his name. . . ."*

"So that's it," said Gladys.

CHAPTER TEN

# *A Sparrow from London*

"Tongkuan has fallen! The Japanese have entered the city...."

"If it's true, we must get out, and quickly...."

"Perhaps it isn't true. You know how these rumours get about."

"It seems true enough this time. We must get ready to leave – you know that was the arrangement. If Tongkuan fell, we must evacuate here immediately."

"Well, we can't do anything tonight. Let's sleep on it, and in the morning we'll know for sure whether Tongkuan has fallen or not."

That seemed wise enough counsel, so that is what they decided to do – the Fishers and the little group of missionaries who were staying with them, including Gladys and her old friend, the Senior Student. It was in 1943, and after another period of comparative inactivity the Japanese were on the march again, drawing nearer and nearer, bombing more and more fiercely.

If they were on the march, then Britishers and Americans were quite sure they must be on the run, away from the invader. There was no question any more about neutrality. Second World War was at its height, and Japan was the enemy of the U.S.A. and Britain, as well as of China. She was the enemy of Norway as well, if it came to that, as Annie Skau was well aware.

Annie was the youngest of the whole group there on the Fisher's mission station, and she was the largest. A regular giantess of a Norwegian was Annie, making even Hubert Fisher look like a slim sapling. She positively towered over Gladys and the Senior Student, chuckling and laughing as the two of them related some of the things that had happened to them since those days in the China Inland Mission's Women's Training Home, when the Senior Student had tried unsuccessfully to coach Gladys for the weekly exams.

Annie was very junior to them all, having only been in China a mere five years, and she was nearly always prepared to do what she was told by her elders and betters. But on this occasion, when morning broke and the Japanese were firmly asserted to be now entrenched in Tongkuan, she was not prepared to pack and make a run for it.

"I do not tink de Lord wants us to go," she confided to Gladys and the Senior Student. "He has spoken to me. He has given me His Word. Look, see what I have been reading . . ." and solemnly she read the words from the little book *Daily Light*, which she held in her hands,

"Behold, I will send a blast upon him, and he shall hear a rumour and return to his own land. . . ."

"De Lord spoke dis to me dis morning, very early," continued Annie. "I was not looking for it – it was in de place where I was reading. I do not tink we should run."

The Senior Student and Gladys looked at each other, and they looked at the text, and they looked at Annie, and slowly they nodded. They knew Annie. She was not given to hasty conclusions arrived at on the spur of the moment. There had been times in their own lives when something they read in the Bible became personal, with a significance that could not be ignored.

"Let's leave the others to get on with their packing," they said. "And let us pray about it." So pray they did, kneeling together the three of them, and as they prayed the conviction deepened that it was going to be all right. This message sent to an Israelitish king thousands of years before somehow became relevant to them in the middle of China in 1943. So relevant, in fact, that they packed nothing at all. "He shall hear a rumour and return . . ."

That is just what happened. The tide of war was already beginning to turn in the Pacific, and the Japanese heard that Americans had landed on one of their islands, so instead of advancing they retreated. That very autumn, instead of being on the run, Annie was back in her old station in the mountains of Shensi, and the Senior Student was continuing her Bible teaching.

Gladys, however, was on the move again. She was still liable to those periods of mental confusion, and the children she had brought out from West of the Mountains were scattered into new homes, into jobs, into the armed forces. There was nothing to hold her in Sian now – perhaps she was restless as a result. When she received an invitation from Dr. and Mrs. Hoyte to stay with them in their home in Lanchow, up in the North-west, the gateway to the long, long routes that led into Central Asia, she accepted.

The clear blue skies of north China spread like a dome over the city whose name she had first heard when she was sitting on a bus in London, reading that little news

item about the first aeroplane to fly from Shanghai to
Lanchow that awakened within her the urge that was to
remain for the rest of her life – the urge towards the
Chinese. Now she was actually here, seeing the place for
herself. Perhaps this would be the place where God
wanted her to serve Him?

The Hoytes lived at the Borden Memorial Hospital on
a barren hillside on the banks of the Yellow River, opposite the great walled city. The hospital was a centre of
healing to which people travelled sometimes for hundreds
of miles. It sprawled along the hillside above the road
that led to Central Asia, along which strings of camels
and heavily laden lorries headed for the deserts. Picturesque Tibetans, Turki men with embroidered skull
caps and leather knee boots, long bearded Muslims whose
women dressed like nuns mingled with the blue clad
Chinese who moved along that road, and passing in and
out through the hospital gates were men and women
whose faces bore the unmistakeable marks of leprosy.
There was plenty to be done, there in the hospital and
in the leprosarium, and everybody on the big compound
was busy. For Gladys there was a home and security.

"Stay with us as long as you like – stay here until you
have really recovered," the Hoytes said to her. But she
was restless still. News reached her of a little town hid in
the mountains where there was a tiny handful of people
who believed in Jesus. They needed someone to teach
them, and there was no-one to go.

"I'll go," said Gladys. Her visit to Lanchow lasted
about a fortnight!

"I did not think she was sufficiently recovered, and

urged her to stay longer," wrote Dr. Hoyte, "but she insisted on leaving at once. . . .

"Whilst she was with us I do not recall any noteworthy incidents or sayings," he continued. "It was what she *did* that made the great impact. She was transparently honest, utterly sincere, her life was completely in harmony with what she said. She was cheerful, never spent time talking about her feelings, her likes or dislikes, and never sought sympathy for her sufferings, was only occupied with how wonderfully God had brought her through, and what kind, good people she had met on her journey through life.

"She was entirely single-minded. She was out to serve God and the Chinese and never thought of herself or her own comfort." Or, as the Senior Student put it once,

"The thing about Gladys is that when she sees a need she plunges straight in," and then she added quietly, "without any thought of the consequences to herself."

So she went south again to a lonely little group in a remote town in the mountains, and spent a hard, cold winter there. The local people were bigotted and resentful, very different from those in her beloved Yangcheng. Women rarely appeared in the streets, and when they did were likely to be cursed by the men, and Gladys had to bear her share of this. She wrote in the margin of that Chinese Bible of hers,
Tsingsui 1944

> Lonely! The very word can start the tears . . .
> > Who walk with Christ can never walk alone.
> Alone, but not alone. He is here. G.A.

There were some things she wrote in the margin of her

Bible to which she put her initials and this was one of them.

She was very poor. The members of the little church provided her with some grain and occasionally a little money, but there were many days when her room was without heat. As always when she was ill at ease, she had little to say and appeared almost unfriendly, and somehow she was not at ease in Tsingsui. She confided to someone later that she was oppressed by the spirit worship that went on in the place, for some of the women were mediums, and there was a sinister atmosphere that disturbed her.

The brightest part of that stay in Tsingsui was the friendship of some of the teenage boys who were there in a refugee school. If the local peasants regarded Ai Weh Teh with suspicion, the young students regarded her with active interest. She was a foreigner, she came from England, she spoke English, and she was prepared to teach them to speak it, too. They crowded into her little room, and when they discovered she had no fire clubbed together to buy some charcoal, huddling together round the pan of glowing coals, listening eagerly to her descriptions of life in her own country. Those mental excursions carried Gladys as well as the boys into realms where facts were lavishly embellished by imagination, and probably did as much to enliven her as her hearers!

She taught them some English sentences, too, and always turned eventually to the Bible, speaking in that compelling way of hers about the Living God Who was calling them to be followers of His Son.

When the boys left, she gave them a little photograph of herself.

To Chu Fu Li,

May you ever be a true soldier of Jesus Christ, and therefore a good citizen of China. G Aylward,

she wrote on the back of one, and gave it to the lad with a letter of introduction to the Senior Student, for he was going near to Sian. And she made a note of his name and address, that she might keep in touch with him, just as she tried to keep in touch with those other "children" of hers, the refugee youngsters from West of the Mountains.

But she could not settle in Tsingsui. This was not the place for her. She went to a neighbouring C.I.M. mission station, and stayed with the resident missionaries for several weeks. It was there that she started talking about Szechwan.

"I'm going to Szechwan," she said. "I feel God wants me in Szechwan."

"It's very different from north China," she was told. "The climate's hotter, and humid. Always cloudy. Dogs bark at the sun down there, the Chinese say! The people of Szechwan are difficult to understand, too – they don't speak our northern Mandarin." But still she talked about going there, although she appeared to do nothing about it. It was only to God she explained that she could not go unless He got her there, since she did not have the money for the ticket.

"If you feel you must go to Szechwan, you'd better go to Chengtu first," the missionaries told her. "There's a C.I.M. Mission Home in the city, and you can go there first until you know what you're going to do." So they bought her a ticket, sent a telegram, saw her off on a ramshackle bus, and she set off for the city, hundreds of miles to the south, for what proved to be her last four years in China.

*        *        *

Sam Jeffery in Chengtu was accustomed to receiving telegrams announcing the imminent arrival of missionaries, known and unknown, so when one was delivered to him with the cryptic message that Gladys Aylward was coming he merely observed, "I've never heard of her before," and passed the message on to his wife so that she would have a bed ready. Gladys arrived in the middle of the night, but that was not unusual, either. That was the time when visitors often turned up. The Jefferys took it philosophically, showed her to her room, told her not to worry about the breakfast bell, she could stay in bed as long as she liked and have something when she had had her sleep out, and left her.

Late the next morning she found her way into the dining room, and as she was eating her breakfast a friendly Englishwoman who was hovering round enquired casually,

"Where do you come from?" It was a common question in those days, when so many refugees were on the move.

"Yangcheng in Shansi," replied Gladys. Four years had elapsed since she left there, but Yangcheng was still home.

"I was in Honan, south of the river till the Japs came," said the other. "Village work. Very different from this great city..."

"Yangcheng was a country place, too," said Gladys. "I don't know what people are talking about here. I heard them talking last night about a jeep and a G.I. What *is* a jeep? What *is* a G.I.?"

"Oh, a jeep is an American all-purpose vehicle that goes over all sorts of rough roads, and a G.I. is an American soldier. Like our British Tommy, you know, only American. Are you planning to stay here in Chengtu, or are you going on somewhere else?" she continued conversationally.

"Don't know," said Gladys shortly. She had no plans to discuss, so what was the use of trying to discuss them? As usual, she had no money, and she did not want to impose on the good nature of complete strangers for longer than necessary. A few days later she announced that she had met a Chinese doctor who was a Christian, and he had offered her a tiny room in the courtyard of his little hospital. There were ways she could help him there, he said. He was needing someone to talk to the patients and preach at his little meetings, so she departed with her few boxes and bundles to revert to an entirely Chinese manner of life.

"How did she get to know people in such a short time here, a complete stranger?" the missionaries asked each other. They met her from time to time, in the street or at church, and noticed that sometimes she behaved strangely, as though her mind were confused. Then the Fishers arrived, with another batch of refugees from Sian, and heard her name mentioned.

"What she needs is plenty of good food," said Mary Fisher briskly. "She'll be all right then. Doesn't look after herself properly. I'll invite her here for a day, shall I?" So it became a regular thing for Gladys to go along to the C.I.M. Mission Home once a week, to have a bath and wash her hair, and have a couple of good meals. And to talk, in English.

Perhaps it was having someone to talk to in her own tongue that meant more to her than anything. "When Mrs. Jeffery knows Gladys Aylward's coming she just puts everything aside and gets out her knitting!" chuckled the young missionaries who were living there while they did their language study. "Mrs. Jeffery knits and smiles, and Gladys talks and talks! It's a life-saver for her."

One day she went along with a large birthday card. "I want you all to sign it," she said. "My mum thinks I'm here all alone, without any friends, and this will cheer her up no end." But after a few hours she disappeared again, back among the Chinese, back to the tiny room with a bed and a table and a chest of drawers and a chair or two – and that huge thermos flask in which to keep hot water to provide her and her guests with drinks for the day.

It was while she was living in the Chinese doctor's courtyard that Jarvis Tien first met her. Jarvis was twenty-two, and had just passed his entrance exam for the Chinese Air Force. He hailed from the province of Yunnan, South of the Clouds, so he was far from home, very poor and very lonely. He went to church more for something to do and somewhere to go than anything else. He had heard the Christian Gospel in Yunnan, though it had made no impression whatever upon him. But a church was a place where you could sit with other people, free of charge, and out of the rain.

It rained a lot in Chengtu. His own mountainous province was bright and sunny, but here in the thickly popu-

110

lated city of Chengtu the air was heavy, the sky seemed always overcast, and it drizzled and drizzled and drizzled.

So Jarvis went to church, and before long his whole attitude towards the Christian Gospel had undergone a complete change, and for the most unlikely reason. It was not through hearing a stirring sermon, or through some devastating mystical experience, but through a simple statement made 2,000 years before by Jesus Christ about birds.

"Behold the fowls of the air," He had said, "for they sow not, neither do they reap, nor gather into barns; yet your Heavenly Father feedeth them."

It is difficult to explain why this made so great an impression on Jarvis. He would have been hard put to it to explain it himself. Like everyone else, he was accustomed to the sight of birds, and took it for granted that they lived in the way they did, without any of the prudence displayed by some of the other creatures, who laid in secret stores for the winter. There was something about the words, "your Heavenly Father feedeth them" that touched him deeply. They seemed to bring God suddenly very near, seeing those perky, twittering little sparrows descending on the ground, pecking around for a moment or two, then sweeping upwards again, obviously without a care in the world. This awareness of God brought about so unexpectedly by the ubiquitous sparrow brought faith to the hitherto unbelieving heart of Jarvis. He became a Christian and was baptized.

Very shortly after that he met Gladys, a sort of little human sparrow with her slightly beak-like nose that took a somewhat wayward course as it travelled down her

111

face, her eyes like black beads, her trim little head thrust eagerly forward and, as he soon discovered, no visible means of support. She spoke to him after one of the services in church, asking his name, where he came from, how long he had been in Chengtu. The lonely young cadet responded shyly, told her about himself, how he had been a teacher in Yunnan, but was now in the Air Force and, furthermore, had become a Christian.

"I've got a book you ought to read," she said. "It'll help you," and she started giving him books, *Pilgrim's Progress* and others. "Jarvis," she said, "You must learn to pray. Prayer is most important in the Christian life. Come along to the prayer meeting."

Christmas drew on. The war in Europe was over now, but the claws of Japan were still dug firmly into China. The economy was in a state of inflation, and money, as soon as it was received, was turned into stores, people buying rice, oil, fuel, cloth, in a frantic effort to invest their money before it lost its value still further. No-one had money in hand for anything other than necessities, but Christmas was Christmas, and could not be allowed to pass without those little exchanges of gifts and greetings that characterise the season of good will among men.

Jarvis, who, like several other young refugee students, was in the habit of going to Gladys' home when he was at a loose end, happened to be there one day when the Chinese pastor, Christian Chang, arrived on his bicycle, jovial and smiling. He had designed some Christmas cards on very cheap paper, and was now making the rounds of his friends, to bring his personal greetings at the Christian festival of the Holy Birth. He gave one to

Gladys, which she received with enthusiasm, and after chatting for a while left his bicycle by her door while he went off to find the doctor and give him a Christmas greeting, too.

When he had gone Jarvis noticed Gladys go to the saddle-bag hanging on the pastor's bicycle, quickly open it, and slip some money inside. Then she fastened it again, and turned away. It was all over in a flash. He knew *that* money was probably nearly all she possessed.

It was strange, the things that made an impression on Jarvis. The flimsy cheap little Christmas card, the warmth and simplicity of the conversation, the swift, secret act of charity were burned indelibly on his memory. "I saw what Christianity really meant," he said many years afterwards, "and Christian giving. I learned this from Ai Weh Teh."

From that time he always went to see her when he had a holiday, and she did what she could to give him a good time, taking him to visit her friends, talking to him about his plans, or just wandering along the streets with him, looking at the things on sale on the stalls or in the little open-fronted shops. When he came along one day and told her he had been selected to go to the U.S.A. for training she promptly started planning. "We must get you in touch with people over there," she said. "Now let me think – the Jefferys! They're American. They'll help." So to the Jefferys she went, demanding letters of introduction for Jarvis, that when he got to America he wouldn't be left on his own. And she gave him a letter addressed to "To Whom It May Concern", to have ready for an unexpected opportunity.

When he was feeling a little lonely in America one day,

he opened it to see what she had said about him and saw she had referred to him as her "adopted son".

That clinched things as far as Jarvis was concerned. He was her son to the end of her life, and that of course gave him the opportunity and the responsibility of doing what he could to help her. His finances flourished in the U.S.A., and from time to time he sent her money.

"I used your gift to have a holiday in the mountains," she wrote to him once, but most of the time the money just went the way money usually went when it was given to Gladys. Like the birds of the air, she did no gathering in barns, for there was always someone under her very nose who needed some food, or clothes, or money for rent; or some young student who couldn't pay his fees.

"It's no use use giving her money," her friends said. "She only gives it away. Same with food. If you take her food you can be sure half of it will have been handed out to someone else before your back is turned!" The best way to ensure that she had a good meal was to sit by her until she had eaten it.

"And she's too trusting!" She helped one young fellow to attend a course in a Bible School, and one day received a letter from him asking for some more money. She could not write well in Chinese, so replied in English, and he had to go to a missionary to get it translated. The missionary, who happened to know him for a rather unsatisfactory student who smoked quite a lot of cigarettes on the quiet, glanced at the letter and then looked at him very straight. There was silence for a moment – a rather significant silence. Then the missionary read the letter to him.

In it Gladys urged him to get on with his studies, and explained that she could not send him any more money, as she was already going without one meal a day to provide him with what she was giving.

# CHAPTER ELEVEN

# *Last Years in China*

Christian Chang drank so much beer and liquor in his youth that he died from cirrhosis of the liver in early middle life. In the period between sowing his wild oats and reaping them in his own body, however, he experienced a transformation of soul which changed the whole course of his residue of years, into which he managed to pack as much service for Jesus Christ as many Christians do in their three score years and ten. That is why he went to a Theological Seminary in Nanking, then to Chengtu, where he was appointed pastor of the big Methodist Church.

It was there that he met Ai Weh Teh, who was a member of the congregation. In her long dark blue Chinese gown and home-made cloth shoes, her hair scraped back from her face, sitting among the Chinese women on their side of the church she looked just like one of them, except for her nose. It soon became evident that she was no ordinary member, though, one who went along to services on Sunday and then disappeared for the rest of the week. She had a way of spotting things that needed to be done, and doing them. She talked to people about God, and it was evident she knew Who she was talking about. And she obviously knew the Chinese manner of life and thought so well that she moved about among them like one of themselves.

She was different from most missionaries, who were either very polite, or very jovial, or very diffident, and almost always smiling, as those who are not quite sure of their acceptance, and want to be friendly. Not so this Ai Weh Teh, who only smiled when there was something to smile about, glared when she was moved to indignation, frowned when she was puzzled (which occurred often in connection with the ramifications of arithmetic) and laughed like a child when she was happy.

She was, in fact, as transparent as water, and her theology was the same, clear and uncomplicated. There was a living God, and she was His servant. There was a loathesome Creature called Satan, and she was his enemy. There was an immortal soul in every human being proceeding to an eternity in either Heaven or Hell. Her job in life was to convince people that if they would but put their trust in Jesus Christ her Lord, who had died on the cross for them, they would get straight on the road to Heaven. And since Jesus Christ had come to life again, and had promised to be with those who trusted and obeyed Him, however beset with trials and temptations the road to Heaven might prove to be, they need fear nothing, for He would never let them down.

Theological Seminaries have a way of making things rather more complicated than that, but when it boiled down to it Christian Chang's theology was really much the same as Gladys', and he was very glad to have her help with some of the things he was doing, such as visiting in prisons. The Chinese Government, the Kuo Min Tang, gave permission freely to propagate religion in their prisons, and Gladys obtained that permission in Chengtu without difficulty.

Very upset she was at times when she emerged. Ai Weh Teh was very tender hearted, as everyone knew. "Oh, that poor fellow in fetters! Oh, Lord, let them take the fetters off! Lord, release him from those fetters, whatever it is that he's done!" When she went again and saw that the fetters had, in fact, been removed, she was over-joyed. "You see, there is a living God, and He answers prayer!" In and out she went, praying and preaching, and as in Yangcheng, so in Chengtu, there were criminals who became convinced to the point of committal that what she told them about Christ was the truth.

When Pastor Christian Chang, therefore, was faced with the necessity of appointing a Biblewoman in the church, he decided that Ai Weh Teh was the one to fit the bill. There were plenty of well educated young Chinese graduates from Bible Colleges who would have accepted the invitation had it been extended to them, but his choice fell on Gladys, and she accepted. She was probably the only westerner ever to be employed in such a capacity in China. She was given a little room behind the big church building, she received the normal allowance given to a Biblewoman, and her status was that of a servant of the church – no more if no less.

One of the jobs that fell to her was cleaning the church, and when she took a look round that gallery it put her on her mettle. What a mess! The dust, and the bits of rubbish, and the general air of neglect and untidiness aroused within her the crusading spirit. This was a challenge to God Himself! Here was His House in a state of disrepair, like when her favourite Bible character, Nehemiah, went to Jerusalem and set about putting things to rights! She tied a towel round her head, and she grasped a brush, and she swept and she tidied, and as she did it she prayed to her God and defied the devil, all in one breath. There was no sitting pretty with a Bible under her arm when there was a battle to be fought, where Gladys was concerned.

"Oh, God, fill this pew on Sunday! Bring the people in to hear Your Word! Beat the devil, Lord, make him loose his clutch on people's souls. Satan, I defy you – in the Name of the Lord get out and stay out!" She sat in a pew and prayed and defied, then she went to the next pew and dusted it, sat and prayed and defied again, all round that gallery, day after day. "Oh, God, bring the people in! Fill this pew on Sunday!"

Probably the beginning of the answer to that prayer was when she met young Hsü the leper. Hsü had been a bank clerk far up in the North-west of China, and when he discovered he had leprosy he was in such despair that he tried to commit suicide. He did not succeed. Instead, like Pastor Christian Chang, he had one of those transforming experiences which changed him from a gloomy, despairing man into one with a purpose in life. He came to Chengtu to a leprosarium connected with the West China Union University, and a dismal place he found it. The trouble was not in the building and the facilities, but with the leprosy patients themselves. They were for ever quarrelling with each other and refusing to obey the rules of the home, and Hsü didn't like the atmosphere at all.

"It's horrible," he told Gladys. "They're all following the devil."

"God can change things," she answered. "God can beat

119

the devil." She pressed her lips together and looked at Hsü, and he looked at her, and they agreed that God could do it, and it was up to them to enter the conflict on His side. So they set about doing it. Gladys went with him into the leprosarium again and again, talking to the men, preaching, telling them about the Living God who had told her to come to China, and doing what she could to help them when they needed something. Faith and good works always went hand in hand where she was concerned.

The outcome was that some of them started going to church on Sundays. They could not sit among other members of the congregation, for the fear of leprosy was too great, but there was the gallery, empty, swept and furnished with benches, and Gladys waiting to lead them up there during the singing of the first hymn. There they sat, with their maimed limbs and distorted faces, out of sight, heads bowed, quietly following the service until they slipped away as the last hymn was being sung.

Good Friday drew near, and Gladys urged that a special Communion service should be arranged for them in the leprosarium. Christian Chang was a little hesitant about taking part at first, but the missionary in charge, Dr. Olin Stockwell, just back from the U.S.A. managed to convince him there was no risk of contagion.

"You lead the service and I'll help you," he said, and so it was arranged. It was an unforgettable occasion as the lepers came slowly forward, some limping, some unable to kneel, some holding out stumps of hands to receive the bread and drink the wine. The atmosphere of the place had been transformed, as Dr. Olin Stockwell

120

observed, and it became an entirely new institution in spirit and practice.

It was while she was living in the little room behind the church that Gladys became "mother" to a lad she named Gordon. She was in great demand among the students because she was willing to teach them English, and a rattling good time they had when she was on that job! "Say it to music," was one of her methods.

> Chengtu will shine tonight
> Chengtu will shine tonight
> When the moon comes up
> And the sun goes down
> Chengtu will shine tonight!

She set it to a tune, and had them all singing it, and when they begged her to do so, gave them English names. This pleased them greatly, and she usually had a group of them around her – and that pleased her!

It was one winter evening, when the room was being prepared for a meeting, that a pressure lamp which Gordon was pumping, exploded. There was a flash, a shriek, then gasps and cries as it was seen that his face and hands had been badly burned. He had to be taken into hospital, seriously injured, and even when he was discharged for convalescence he could do nothing for himself. His hands were still useless.

At this stage Gladys took over completely. She did everything for him. He had been living with an uncle who was very unkind to him, but now he was on the church compound, and Gladys was his "mother". Gradually he was nursed back to health, his hands completely restored, and Gordon, a gentle shy teenager, was a committed

Christian. When Gladys went out to preach in some courtyard, or went off to a nearby village, Gordon went with her. She wrote to Jarvis, now in the U.S.A., about her youngest son Gordon, his zeal, and his devotion to the Lord. The time came when she was very ill, lying in her little room, sometimes delirious, and it was Gordon then who did everything for her.

"He was the only one who could quieten me," she told a friend. "I'd rave, and insist on getting up, and then he'd come along and say, 'Now, mother, don't be impatient. Just lie quietly,' and he'd stay beside me till I dropped off to sleep." Word eventually got to the Stockwells that she was ill, and they carried her off to their home until she recovered. Gordon used to go along there, rather shyly, to visit her, and as he left she would go outside with him and they would pray together in the still of the night. There was a tenderness in that relationship between the woman in her mid-forties and the lad who was still not twenty which touched those who saw it. Gladys had several "adopted sons" in the course of her life, but none more dear than Gordon.

Meanwhile, China's short lived period of peace after the war was disturbed by ominous news from the north of the country. The Communists were emerging from their lair in Yenan with a steel-like discipline and a dedication before which nothing seemed able to stand.

"It looks as though they'll take over eventually," westerners in China said. "But of course, it'll take them years to do it – ten years at least. . . ." But the news from the north began to belie this optimism, and there were rumours of wealthy Chinese families pulling out of China while the going was good. When the few missionaries

who were scattered in the city of Chengtu met from time
to time, they talked about it.

"We'll stay, of course," they said, "But it'll be difficult.
If our Consuls begin badgering us to leave we'll just have
to ignore them. We must stay. The Christians are going
to have a hard time of it. . . ." And then, as they talked,
they thought about Gladys Aylward.

"Wish we could get her out of it," they said. "It's all
very well for us to stay on – after all, our Governments
will ask awkward questions if anything happens to us.
But she's a naturalised Chinese now. If the Communists
got control here and arrested her, we couldn't do a thing.
. . . Not a thing. Wish we could get her out of it."

Dr. Olin Stockwell cautiously broached the subject to
Gladys herself. Her job in the church had been changed,
and she was now appointed to visit the smaller churches
that lay between Chengtu and Chungking, which took
her out of the city for several weeks at a time. When she
returned, it was to the Stockwells' home that she went,
and she had become a personal friend.

"It was always a joy to have her," they said. "Her over-
flowing joy and laughter and spiritual life, and her ability
to adjust to every situation, made her a delightful guest."
But she was in no way their responsibility, and they knew
that to suggest she should get out of China merely to save
her own skin would probably have the reverse effect. So
Dr. Stockwell merely asked her how many years it was
since she left home, and didn't she think it was about
time she went on leave? She agreed that she'd been out
for about seventeen years, and her parents were old and
she'd like to see them again – but she had no money. How-

123

ever, she said, she would pray about it, and if the Lord wanted her to go, she would go.

While she prayed, therefore, Dr. Stockwell got busy. He wrote first to the Orphaned Missions Committee. This was an organization that had been set up by the major missionary societies in China during the war to find support for German missionaries and others who were cut off from their home countries. He told the Committee that he had an "orphan missionary" who ought to return to England, and when he explained who it was, they agreed to pay her boat fare from Shanghai. Then he asked the China Inland Mission to provide her board and room at their headquarters in Shanghai while she was there, and that, too, presented no difficulty. There remained the air passage from Chengtu to Shanghai, but he had a fund for evangelistic work from which to draw, and if Gladys Aylward hadn't done her share of evangelistic work, he didn't know who had! He paid for the air ticket out of the funds and never had a qualm of conscience over it, not even during the nine months when the Communists had him "confessing his sins".*

Getting out of China proved even more complicated for Gladys than getting into it. She had to obtain a Chinese passport and that involved going to Nanking before she ever got to Shanghai. Arriving there, further formalities awaited attention, for an alien could not enter Great Britain on the same terms as a citizen, and sponsorship papers were required, involving the business manager at the China Inland Mission in many a journey to various officials to get everything properly arranged.

* Dr. Olin Stockwell was imprisoned in China for two years, from November, 1950 to November 1952.

Gladys herself was scarcely aware of it, however, for she had her time cut out getting in touch with some of the youngsters she had met elsewhere. Just as years before, among the swarms of refugees, groups of schoolchildren and university students had moved from east to west China to evade the Japanese, now they were moving to the coast, to evade the advancing Communists. The little island of Taiwan had been ceded back to China from the Japanese after the war, and it was to Taiwan that many were going now. The exodus had started. Mukden had already fallen to the Communists, and although it was not until 1 October 1949 that General Mao Tse-Tung officially proclaimed the People's Republic of China, the writing was on the wall as far as the Chinese Nationalist Government was concerned. The great port of Shanghai saw more going than coming in those days, as ship after ship drew out, laden with Chinese who were leaving the land of their fathers for ever.

Among them were some of the students Gladys had known in the western provinces, and with whom she had contrived to maintain a link by correspondence. One of these lads was amazed, one day, to see a letter addressed to himself stuck up on the notice board of the place where he was staying, written by Ai Weh Teh, asking him to come and see her at an address in Sinza Road. What was Ai Weh Teh doing in Shanghai? He went along to Sinza Road in a large compound with great, four-storied buildings, where she was staying at the China Inland Mission headquarters.

She greeted him eagerly. He was going to Taiwan? She was going to England. God had provided her with a ticket. Indeed, He was providing for her all the way along the line, like He always had done. Only that day she had gone along to the reception desk, and there in her pigeon-hole was an anonymous gift of U.S. $10! When her young visitor left she gave him an electric torch, and a silver dollar, and he wasn't the only one, either. Those young people, her "children", she might never see them again, and she must do all she could for them while she could. Little wonder if she was practically penniless as the time drew near for her to board the vessel that would take her to England when, one day, she had an unaccountable urge to go to the Hongkong and Shanghai Bank.

She did not know how to get there, but someone from the C.I.M. offered to go with her. Thinking she was going to draw out money, her companion on arrival naturally led her to the appropriate counter, but Gladys looked dazed, and said, "No, I have to meet someone who works here." That was all she knew.

Her companion, somewhat perplexed, went to the lift man for help. He ushered them into the lift and let them out at the first floor, into a large room with about fifty desks, at all of which people seemed to be working.

"Can you see the person you want?" Gladys was asked. She continued to look dazed. She did not know who she wanted to see. All she could say was,

"The Lord told me to come here to see someone."

Then suddenly, a tall young Chinese, smartly dressed, came quickly towards her, smiling broadly and holding out his hand.

"Miss Aylward! What are you doing here? Where are you going?" he asked. She looked at him blankly.

"I'm one of your 'children,'" he said. "You don't recognise me, do you?" Then he told her his name, and her face lit up.

"I'd never have known you! Why, you've grown so tall . . .!" They chatted together happily for a minute or two, then he asked again,

"What are you doing here in Shanghai? Where are you going?" And when she told him he said "Then if I may I should like to give you something for your travelling expenses," and forthwith proceeded to do so.

The Chinese are very generous on such occasions....

# CHAPTER TWELVE

# In the Ascendant

Gladys Aylward's rise to fame is one of the strangest "success stories" of the twentieth century. When Dr. Handley Stockley was once asked why she hadn't died as a result of that terrible illness in Sian following the trek with the children over the mountains, he answered rather quietly, "I can only think it is because God has other work for her to do." It is difficult to find any other explanation than a supernatural one for the fact that her name can be grouped with people like Dr. Albert Schweitzer and Helen Keller, and known to millions who never went inside a church except to get married.

When she arrived back in England in the Spring of 1949 she looked so small and insignificant that her own parents did not recognise her. They had gone to the London terminus to meet her off the boat train, and hurried up and down searching for her in vain. Not until responding to an announcement over the loudspeaker requesting those who had come to meet Miss Gladys Aylward from China to go to the stationmaster's office did they realise that the bewildered little Chinese woman standing there with a miscellaneous assortment of bags and bundles was their daughter. As for Gladys, she looked without recognition at the bright-eyed little elderly woman a-sparkle with diamante ornaments who hurried towards her.

"My Mum had come all out in diamonds!" she said later when describing her reactions to Mum's gallant efforts to brighten the austere fashions of post-war Britain. In her confusion she talked in a mixture of Chinese and English, complained rather irritably of the cramped conditions in the little home in Cheddington Road, stared blank and unsmiling when introduced to Violet's husband. There seemed no place for her here in England, where she was now in the "alien" category, and had to go along to the police station to report periodically. Everything was strange, and she thought longingly of the old, familiar life in China.

She soon found there was plenty for her to do, however, for Mum was an unofficial, unconscious publicity agent of the first order. A regular little gad-about in a thoroughly respectable way was Mum. She was glad to get out and leave the running of the house to Violet, for she was in great demand as a speaker at women's meetings, a prime favourite down Hoxton way, and liable to turn up at all sorts of church functions unimpeded by any denominational barriers. "Our Gladys in China" had been her subject for many an address and many a conversation, and when, in the course of her peregrinations, she ran into the well-known journalist, Hugh Redwood, author of the best-seller *God in the Slums*, he began writing about her. So one way and another, invitations to speak at church meetings began rolling in as soon as it was known that Mrs. Aylward's daughter was back from China. And Hugh Redwood inserted a little paragraph in the London daily of which he was the night editor, to the effect that a Miss Gladys Aylward had returned to England after seventeen years' missionary work in China. It took about a couple of lines of small print.

Now it so happened that about that time a B.B.C. producer was working on a dramatized series of true stories for the B.B.C., called *The Undefeated*. His name was Alan Burgess, and as he was always on the lookout for copy, he made a point of glancing through the papers for any likely clues. When he saw that some woman who had been for a very long time in China was back in England he made a note of it. Might be a story there somewhere. He'd go along and see her some time.

When he eventually made his way to Cheddington Road, Edmonton, and knocked at the well-polished knocker of No. 67, it was Gladys who opened the door. She was alone in the house, and when the young man on the doorstep explained that he was from the B.B.C., was producing real life radio plays, and wondered if she would grant him an interview, she said immediately oh no, certainly not. He pleaded a little, and although she asserted that nothing had ever happened to her worth making into a play, she relented towards him. After all, he looked a nice young man. In some ways Gladys never quite grew up. She was always rather susceptible to nice young men, and this one looked disappointed, and uncomfortably warm. It was a hot day.

"Come in and have a cup of tea," she said. "I'll show you a real Chinese tea-box – a sort of tea cosy." And while he sat down by the table she went out into the scullery, put on the kettle, and produced the tea-box into which the teapot could be stowed and it would keep hot for hours and hours.

With the contrariness of human nature Gladys, renowned among her friends for her stories of personal experiences, with which she had been known to hold up many a meal-time, closed right down at the prospect of having them reported. She seemed determined to keep the conversation centred on the tea-box.

"You must have had many strange experiences in China," the young man ventured. Gladys admitted she had, but doubted whether people would be interested in any of them. "Now just look and see how this thing works! Much better than a tea cosy ..." It took Alan Burgess at least a quarter of an hour to get anything out of her, but after persistent though cautious questioning he elicited the information that she had once taken some children across the mountains in north China.

How long did it take her?

A month or so.

How much money did she have?

Money? She didn't have any money!

How many children?

She didn't know exactly, about a hundred.

"I see," said Burgess. What he saw was not how she had done it, but that he had struck journalistic oil, that this unassuming little woman in her queer get-up had a most remarkable story. It might take him several journeys out to Edmonton to get it, but he knew they would prove to be worth it.

The half-hour dramatization of her story was produced that autumn on the B.B.C., and it was a hit. The following spring a paper booklet appeared in the religious bookshops entitled *Gladys Aylward ... One of the Un-defeated*.* But by the time it appeared she was already widely known as a speaker.

She made people sit up – literally! The Rev. the Hon. Roland Lamb noticed this when he invited her to speak, soon after her arrival at an afternoon meeting largely attended by elderly ladies. The usual preliminaries over, the cup of tea partaken of, the time came for the address to be given. The speaker stood up, a very small, rather odd-looking woman in a funny Chinese gown, and the elderly ladies settled back on their chairs, prepared to take it easy for the next twenty minutes. One or two of them closed their eyes. They were ready for a nap.

"And God said to Abraham," started the speaker. Then she suddenly shouted,

"GET OUT!" The elderly ladies shot up in their seats, eyes wide open with alarm. For the next hour they sat, eyes glued to the speaker, time forgotten, as she related the things that had happened when the same message from God had come to her as had come to Abraham – "Get out from your own country...."

At the time when I went to China I was the most unlikely person to do anything, let alone go to China. I had never passed an examination. Me go to China? Gladys Aylward, I said, why you? You've never even passed an examination...

But God wasn't asking me if I could read properly. He was saying,

"Gladys Aylward, would you allow Me to open your ears and your mouth, and let me drop in Chinese?

* Told by her to R. O. Latham. Published by Edinburgh House Press.

Because it's to these people I want you to prove My
glory and tell of My salvation...."

"Friends, if God ever worked a miracle in this whole
wide world, He worked one in my head. I speak
Chinese! Oh, I do! But don't think I am proud. I am
only humble before a great Almighty God Who says,
'When I call, I will equip.' And He does. You just have
to say, 'Well, here I am. You just do what you like
with me.'"

There were those alarming duties of the early months
in China, when Jeannie Lawson decided to open an inn
for muleteers in order to preach to them....

... She was the old Scots woman who I should say
was the drawing power to get me to China. We opened
a new inn. Now don't think I opened the inn! No, I
didn't. I would never have had anything to do with
mules if Jeannie hadn't forced me. No, I certainly
wasn't in love with mules! But you know, you get into
corners and you just have to go forward, that's all.

I have tried to think sometimes, I wonder what
would have happened if when I was outside the door,
perspiring all over, grumbling and grousing in my
heart, waiting for those mules to come up the road,
and I was supposed to grab them in.... Well, suppos-
ing I hadn't grabbed them in!

Oh, the awful thought! At least one man would not
be in eternity with the Lord of Glory....

There were so many things she had to tell about the
children. One of those she had taken in at Yangcheng,
for instance, who wandered out into the street and met

a little beggar boy, complete with his begging bowl and stick to beat off the dogs, and asked him....

"What have you got in your bowl?"

"Nothing."

"Got any money?"

"No."

"Had anything to eat today?"

"No."

"I have! Ate to the full on porridge and bread this morning. Ate to the full on noodles for dinner." Pause. "Where did you sleep last night?"

"Under a wall outside the city."

"That's where I used to sleep." (Then, in a tone of deep satisfaction) "I don't sleep there now, though! See those gates over there?"

"Yes. I see them."

"That's where I live now. Eat to the full every day there.... You can come and live there if you like...."

She had the elderly ladies laughing one minute, crying the next, and when they left the hall, fifty minutes later than usual, they were telling each other they could have gone on listening for hours.

For the next twenty years she went on telling those stories. The exploits of Gladys Aylward were her stock in trade. She ruthlessly exposed the things "that silly little Gladys Aylward" had done, and the wonderful way the Living God had worked in spite of her stupidity. When most of the epics of the Second World War had been published and forgotten, hers continued to hold her audience like a spell. She started her career as a speaker in a small way, back in 1949, at week-day meetings in inconspicuous churches, and was quite likely to be found

sitting on the kerb somewhere in the vicinity, taking a
rest, a bag beside her containing a few Chinese curios and
her Chinese Bible. That Bible accompanied her everywhere, held together in places with strips of sticky tape
and freely marked with underlinings and notes in the
margins. She was convinced that some of them were messages from God to her – Luke 21 : 15, for instance, alongside which she had written while waiting in Shanghai her
own free translation – "I will give you eloquence" and
noted under it "Promise for journey, March 1949."

That promise was speedily fulfilled, and in an in-
credibly short time she was receiving invitations to speak
to larger audiences.

The first time she knew that the local mayor would be
present, complete in his regalia, she was somewhat dis-
mayed, and tempted to get out of the arrangement. She
didn't want to move among the nobs, she said. But then
she took herself to task.

"Gladys," she demanded sternly, "Hasn't *he* got a
soul?" So she went, and before long she was taking
mayors in her stride, and bishops too, for that matter.
After all, they were nothing more and nothing less than
human beings with immortal souls. If Nehemiah, her
hero, when he was butler to Artaxerxes king of the Medes
and Persians had referred to his master merely as "this
man," she need not be abashed by bishops. And when
one or another of them shared the platform with her, and
saw her rapier-like technique of whirling on her audience
in the middle of one of her stories with the challenge,
"Will you search your hearts and see if you are willing
to obey this wonderful God?", sensed the awe and the

Presence as people sat breathless, and here and there tears began to flow....

Well, the bishops who knew themselves to be but mere men were the first to acknowledge that it was usually the parlourmaid who stole the thunder.

As for Gladys herself, she went along to the meetings in a very matter-of-fact way, as though she were going to her daily work. She travelled everywhere by public transport, and had her little grumble, "Keep having to say the same thing over and over again – makes me feel like a gramophone record!" When money began to roll in from the collections that were given to her its destination was obvious. It rolled on towards China. The missionaries in Chengtu had quite a time of it trying to understand her muddled instructions, distributing the money to the best of their ability, though sometimes against their better judgment. Young Gordon Wang was acquitting himself well as an assistant pastor, but not all the recipients of her gifts were like him! She kept up a correspondence with as many of her Chinese friends as possible, and assured them that she was hoping to return soon.

They replied guardedly. Then the news began to filter through of the reign of terror under the Communists, as they gained full control, with the secret arrests and the long indoctrinations, the interrogations and the accusation meetings at which brother betrayed brother, and the mass executions in public places.

The horror of it preyed upon her mind, and on one occasion, when she happened to be sharing a room with a friend, she was unable to sleep, moaning and crying in her distress.

"It's my children," she wept brokenly. "Something awful is happening. They're in danger – I know it!" It was as though she was fey, enduring the mental agony of one appointed to death. Her body trembled and she was bathed in perspiration as they knelt down together, praying through the hours of the night for Ninepence and Less and Liang and Gordon, and dozens of others.

"I'm going back to China," she said. "I must get back to them." But about that time a letter reached her from far inland China. It was couched in unusual language, explaining that if she came back she would not need much – only six feet of ground and a strip of cloth. And if she went back some whom she knew there would only need six feet of ground and a strip of cloth, too.

Her presence would make things even worse for the very people she wanted to help, for she was already suspected as being a spy for the Imperialists.

She knew it was the end, as far as returning to China was concerned. But it wasn't the end as far as the Chinese were concerned. There were Chinese in London, restaurant keepers and laundry workers, and smart young students, too, from Hong Kong and the Malaysian peninsula. She heard of a Pastor Stephen Wang, a refugee from China who was starting to hold Sunday services for Chinese people, and she wrote to him saying she would like to help him. He welcomed her, and when she was in London on a Sunday she went along to the services, and in the meetings at which she spoke talked about the work among Chinese in London.

"They want you to go along and tell them about it, Pastor Wang!" she said enthusiastically, and began making arrangements for him to travel to various parts of England in order to do it. She was rather irritated when he demurred. As he said, his job was to hunt up the lonely Chinese in London, and help them. If he spent his time going around talking about what he was doing, he would have no time left to do what he was talking about.

It was a logic with which she could not but agree, and was inclined to act upon it herself, when the need of an individual conflicted with the timing of a meeting. The individual must come first! A couple of days before one big meeting at which she was due to speak the organising committee received a little note from her to say that she was very sorry, she would not be able to come. The committee was thrown into a state of panic. The notices were out, coach loads of people from the surrounding neighbourhood were coming to hear Miss Gladys Aylward, the famous woman missionary, and now she wasn't coming.

"Can you possibly help us – can you persuade her to come?" they pleaded with a friend of hers who happened to be in the district. So she put through a long distance phone call, and when Gladys answered it, started off,

"Look here, Gladys, about this meeting you're supposed to be coming to the day after tomorrow ..."

"Yes, I know, I'm sorry about that," said Gladys airily. "But there's someone I *must* see that evening."

Some Chinese I suppose, thought her friend, though she didn't say so.

"But this meeting – they've advertised it – crowds of people are coming."

"I'm sorry," said Gladys firmly. "I can't come – someone's passing through London that night, and they're going on next morning early, and I *must* see them."

"But Gladys, you can't do this sort of thing. You *said* you'd come!" Then, with a flash of inspiration, she added, "Let your yea *be* yea, and your nay, nay."

There was a brief pause at the other end of the line. Gladys knew who had first said that: Jesus Christ her Lord in the Sermon on the Mount.

"All right – I'll come," she said. Then she added quickly, "But I must get back to London that night. I can't stay – I must get back."

"There's a train at eight-thirty, and I'll see you catch it – if you can stop speaking at twenty past," was the prompt reply. "It's up to you!" It was well known that Gladys never spoke for less than one hour, but on that occasion she confined herself to forty-five minutes, and caught the train.

Many were the stories her hostesses had to tell about her. The way, for instance, she would sometimes leave little gifts of food secreted in homes where she felt her presence might have added strain to the family exchequer. One hostess found a packet of bacon under the bed a fortnight after Miss Aylward had left! In another home there was anxiety about a member of the family who was always going off to the public house, and returning the worse for drink. He was there on the evening when Gladys was to arrive, and she found her hostess nearly in tears. Gladys pursed her lips. This was a challenge, and she accepted it.

"We'll get him out!" she said. "We'll *pray* him out!" and she forthwith proceeded to do so.

"Lord, get him out!" she prayed, her fists clenched.

"Lord – make his beer taste 'orrible. Make him hate the taste of it. Tell him to push it away from him across the counter...

"Lord, make him get up off that stool. Bring him over to the bar door.... Make him push it open and come outside.... Bring him across the road... Make him walk along the street, back home...."

There was a sound at the front door. The prodigal had returned! And to Gladys as well as her hostess, that mattered a lot more than the fact that the evening meeting was packed to the doors.

Within a year of her return to England she was in constant demand, travelling far and wide, often returning to London so late at night that to get home to Edmonton involved arriving in the early hours of the morning if she missed the last train. As in China, so in England – there were always the people who said, "There's a bed for you any time you like, Gladys."

One of these was the assistant in Bethany. Bethany was a sort of refuge for women run by Sister Gemmel of the Church Army in a basement flat at Marble Arch, and Miss Bralant helped her. Gladys soon had a nickname for Miss Bralant. "The Coolie" she called her once, laughing, and the name stuck. "I've got a couple of rooms in a house not far from here," said the Coolie. "There are two beds in my bedroom – you're very welcome to come there any time you like. I'm out most of the time, so I'll give you a key."

The claims of Bethany kept the Coolie from her two rooms in Westbourne Park all day and much of the night, but she returned late one evening and realised Gladys had been there. The place was very clean and very tidy, as Gladys always left it, and on the table was a little piece of paper torn from a small notebook, on which was some pencilled scribbling in Gladys' rather childish handwriting. The Coolie picked it up and read:

"Thank you dear. It needs no more than that from me, for *He* will reward you.

I have loved the quiet.

I will come some other time even when I have not a meeting.

Will let you know,

Yours, Gladys.

Isa. 53 : 1–12. I love it all."

The Coolie was touched. It was she who had shared the room with Gladys on that night when she had been almost fey, agonising over her "children" in China. She had heard some of the inner conflicts of those lonely years, some of the sufferings and humiliations. She had seen the little figure in the simple Chinese dress lugging a big bag through the London streets and down into the Underground setting off for a round of meetings when she was feeling too tired to bother to get herself a proper meal. She couldn't do much for Gladys, but she was glad she had two little rooms up on the third floor of a rather shabby house near central London to share with her when she needed them. She read on, and suddenly became aware that she was standing on holy ground. Gladys had finished her note of thanks with the words,

"In your quiet room I have renewed my vow to follow all the way."

The Coolie was a tidy person, not given to hoarding, throwing out old magazines relentlessly and tearing up letters as soon as she had answered them. But she could never bring herself to throw away that scrap of paper, on which Gladys had written her "thank you" letter.

# CHAPTER THIRTEEN

# The Small Woman

The half-hour dramatisation of Gladys' story on the B.B.C. in 1949 was such a hit that it was decided to reproduce it two or three years later. And since it was known that Miss Aylward was still in England, it was agreed that the programme would be strengthened if she herself would add a short epilogue in her own words and her own voice. Alan Burgess went along to see her about this, procured the recording, the programme was duly produced again, and that might have been the end of it, had it not been that a publisher happened to tune in at the time it was on, and listened right through to the end.

A few days later he put through a telephone call to Alan Burgess.

"I want you to write a book about that woman," he said.

"Nothing doing," was the prompt reply. "I've written five books already, and got less than £400 for the lot! Nothing doing! No money in writing books."

"I'll pay you £400 down if you'll take it on," persisted the publisher. Burgess remained unenthusiastic. However, he eventually agreed to go and see Gladys and find out if she would be willing to provide him with the material. She's pretty sure to say no, he said to himself.

To his surprise, she agreed immediately. She thought a

book would be a very good idea. She happened to know
that the booklet produced after the first broadcast was
still selling like ice cream in summer at the religious bookshops. (It went into seventeen impressions within eight
years.) What she wanted, however, was that this new
book should be written for an even wider reading public
than had been reached already. The more people who
knew what God had done for her, the better.

"I didn't want to write that book," Alan Burgess admitted years later. Don't know why I did it." Then he
added, "I suppose I just had to...."

Getting the material involved him in interviews with
Gladys nearly every day over a period of about four
months. By this time she was sharing a little house in a
mews near Marble Arch with Mrs. Rosemary Tyndale
Biscoe. The two of them had met after one of Gladys'
meetings, and as Rosemary had come to a cross-roads in
her life, Gladys said casually, "You can come and live
with me if you like. I've just got a little place in a mews."
So Rosemary went and lived with her, and soon discovered that Gladys' main concern in life was getting
clothes and money sent to refugees escaping from Communist China in Hong Kong. Some of the missionaries
Gladys had known in China, including Annie the young
Norwegian giantess, were right there, doing what they
could to help them. Gladys had a way of inspiring people
to action, and many of her friends, including Queenie
(married and with her own family now, but still devoted
to her cousin), helped in the collecting of unwanted
clothes to send out to the refugees.

Into this work of sorting, packing and posting Rosemary threw herself. She came originally from that

stratum of English society where other people did the packing, but what she lacked in experience she made up for in enthusiasm. There were times when Gladys looked round in despair and fled for refuge to the Coolie in Bethany. "Rosemary's got so many clothes and packages and bundles everywhere I can't get into the place!" she complained. The Coolie smiled soothingly and made her a cup of tea. She thought it wiser not to mention that a day or two previously Rosemary had been round, almost in tears because Gladys had got the place so filled with Chinese she couldn't get on with the packing....

On one occasion Gladys went to Belfast to speak, and returned with an inarticulate little Chinese widow. Wang Kwei had been brought from Hong Kong as a nanny, landed up in a mental hospital where no one could understand her, since she spoke no English, and where she might have remained till her dying day had Gladys not gone security for her and brought her back to London. She lived in the house in the mews for about a couple of years and eventually returned, hale and hearty, to her family in Hong Kong.

Into the house in the mews went Alan Burgess, picking his way over parcels and bundles of clothing to sit down with Gladys and delve into her memory for material for people who didn't go to church, as well as those who did. She took it all quite seriously, determined to give him a true picture of her life in Yangcheng, with the consequence that day after day he was escorted on preaching trips to the villages in the wake of Gladys, complete with a roll of Gospel posters and her Bible. He did not know much about missionaries. He felt he knew enough however to conclude that a woman missionary going out to

145

a village to preach was in the same category as a dog biting a man when it came to making news. They were simply doing what might be expected of them. Not until the man bites the dog is Fleet Street interested, and not until Gladys did something else than go off to a village to preach would there be anything for him to write about. It was extremely difficult to deflect her from this course of action, and he had to listen patiently, his experienced ear cocked for any word that might lead to a real story.

One such came when, as usual, she was preparing to go out to a village with Mr. Lu, the evangelist, but was delayed for a few hours by trouble in the prison. However, they got away at last, and she had the two Ways Poster with her....

Prison! The journalist stiffened in his chair at the magic word. Prison! A village isn't news, but a prison is!

"Hold on a minute, Gladys," he said. "What was that about the prison?"

"Oh, they stopped me just as we were going out to the village."

"Who stopped you?"

"The people from the prison."

"But why?"

"There was a riot in the prison." Then she added scornfully, "Silly things!"

"But what had that to do with you?"

"The Governor wanted us to go and stop it."

"They wanted you to....! Well, did you?"

"Yes."

Whew! And he might have missed it! Burgess leaned forward and said firmly,

"Now Gladys, I want you to tell me about that riot in the prison. Never mind about preaching in the village – tell me about that riot in the prison."

So she told him. The gist of it was that one of the prisoners had got hold of a hatchet and was rushing round with it, hacking people, and the rest of them were milling around, fighting each other. The Governor, appalled by the din, was afraid to go in himself, and had sent for her because, as he reminded her, she was always preaching about the Living God Who was with her, and if He was with her she ought to be able to quell the riot. So Gladys, put on her mettle, went in, demanded that the man with the hatchet give it to her at once, which he did, and then gave them all a scolding for being so silly. Burgess, stifling his amazement, quickly asked her questions to fill in the background for what he realised would be one of the highlights in the book. He had to get them, and he had to get them *now*, before she went off to preach in that village!

So it went on. When he had got from her as much as she could remember of those first few years in China, he said,

"Well, Gladys, I'll write this up, and we'll go halves on whatever we get for it. There's £200 apiece for us now, and we'll see what else comes in." A legal document to this effect was duly drawn up and signed by them both, he went away to sort the material and write *The Small Woman*, and Gladys to continue that ever-widening circle of meetings, arranged for by an ever-widening circle of friends. For Gladys made friends wherever she went. She was a popular guest, easy to please, full of humour, and always a favourite with the children. There seemed

147

to be an instinctive mutual attraction between them, and when headmasters of schools knew she was in the neighbourhood they urged her to come and speak about China. They soon discovered, however, that they must be prepared for an alteration in the normal schedule. It was useless to expect Miss Aylward to confine herself to fifteen minutes at Assembly! Even the headmaster at Gordonstoun discovered this. An Air Commodore and his wife who knew Gladys well, and to whom they had given the key of their large West-end apartment to go in and out as she liked, introduced her at Gordonstoun when the young heir to the throne was a pupil there. A few weeks before Gladys went, His Royal Highness the Duke of Edinburgh had gone there to speak to the boys, and the Principal had respectfully warned him that no one could hold their attention for more than twenty minutes.

If he told Gladys the same thing, it made no difference. She spoke for about an hour and a quarter, and the boys listened spellbound. The headmaster said it had never happened before, in all his long experience of boys. Later, at another well-known public school after she had spoken to the boys and was having dinner in the headmaster's private quarters where no boy was ever allowed to go unless invited, the manservant approached the headmaster to announce that a group of boys was at the front door asking if they could speak with Miss Aylward. That was the end of the dinner party as far as Gladys was concerned, for the boys were nothing more and nothing less than human beings with immortal souls, whether they came from the British aristocracy, the mountains of China or the Welsh valleys.

One of those boys was asked, years later, what it was about her that impressed him, and after a moment's thought he answered, "It was the way she talked about God – as though she knew Him ..."

In 1957 *The Small Woman* was published by Evans Brothers Ltd., and Twentieth Century-Fox Films wanted to dramatise it. Alan Burgess said to Gladys,

"What about it, Gladys? Shall we let them make a film of it?"

Yes, she thought it would be a good idea. It would be a way of reaching more people. It did not occur to her that everything would not be produced just as she liked it, that she would not be invited to choose the cast and control the script writing.

She thought it would all be just like it was with the editor of the *Sunday Companion* who was so interested in her plans to return to the Far East.

For that was what she was intending to do now, The one person who she could not have hurt by leaving England again had died. Bright-eyed, vivacious little Mum's earthly pilgrimage had ended. Mum, with her saucy, gay, defiant little home-made hats and her impish ways, her Cockney wit that had her listeners rocking with laughter till her sudden transitions to the cross where Jesus died stilled and melted them – Mum was gone.

"I promised her once that I wouldn't go back while she was alive," Gladys told Violet. "But I'm free to go now. I'm going back."

She set sail for Hong Kong in April 1957, after putting her signature to the agreement whereby the film rights of *The Small Woman* were granted to Twentieth Century-Fox Films.

# CHAPTER FOURTEEN

# *In Orbit*

The next four years of Gladys' life, viewed in retrospect, are like a series of whirlwinds in which she was carried to dizzy heights, then plunged to terrifying depths as she trod the perilous path of fame and notoriety. There were occasions when her cabin on a liner looked like that of a film star as she set off on one of her tours, gay and fragrant with baskets and bouquets of flowers, and her arrival was liable to be announced over the radio as a piece of current news. She was one of the people at whom press photographers quickly raised their cameras when she appeared in a crowd attending a function. But in those undated, unpunctuated, jumbled letters of hers to Queenie she wrote,

"You know I didn't want all this hoo-hah! I'm still the same Gladys you knew when we went together into the gallery at Drury Lane," and on another occasion, "I've got two photographs I don't know who will want so I'll send one to you and one to the Coolie. It's a picture of me and the Arch." As Gladys was in Hong Kong, Queenie looked forward to seeing a picture of Gladys standing in an oriental setting under an elaborate arch, but when it arrived the "Arch" turned out to be the Archbishop of Canterbury.

Floods of letters reached her. A suitcase of unanswered

correspondence seemed part of her baggage. She became
involved in the business side of running orphanages and
mission halls which revealed over and over again that
basic weakness in arithmetic which the best efforts of her
teachers in the primary school in Edmonton had failed
to rectify. Her most devoted admirers had to admit that
she had no head for business, and in the course of the
tumultuous years those who tried to manage her affairs
were sometimes hard put to it to understand her instructions and interpret her silences.

As for her close personal friends, they held their breath
many a time for quite another reason. It was not only
that they did not know what Gladys would do next –
they were afraid of what she would say next. It is one
thing to talk freely when you are an ordinary person of
no importance. It is quite another thing to talk freely
when you are a public figure whose words are likely to
be reported in the press. Interesting news items appeared
from time to time reporting that Miss Gladys Aylward,
the tiny woman missionary of China, now had another
fight on her hands. She had taken on the giants of Hollywood over the filming of "The Inn of the Sixth Happiness." What she said about them was whittled down to a
few terse but colourful sentences of an inflammatory
nature. She learned to avoid press conferences, with their
cross-examinations that so easily elicited from her the
wrong answers, or things she would not have said except
in confidence.

Some of the things she wrote would have had even
greater news value if they had got into print. Fortunately,
she confined most of them to letters to her friends, to
whom she wrote without inhibition. Queenie used to keep

those that came to her in a special box, to lend to people who helped her in collecting and dispatching clothes to Hong Kong refugees. It helped to maintain their interest, to read for themselves what Gladys was doing. There were times, however, when Queenie's face grew very alarmed as she perused the latest epistle from Gladys, and on thinking it over she decided not to add it to the pile in the box. It might get into the wrong hands! So she took it quietly out into the kitchen and consigned it to the flame instead. It seemed the safest thing to do. Better have nothing in her possession to provide evidence in the event of Gladys being sued for libel!

When she was on the platform her power to move her audiences was amazing. Her artless descriptions of her own experiences, her realistic "conversations" with God, her direct challenge to her listeners to a life of faith and sincerity had its effect on old and young, rich and poor, simple and intellectual alike. The well-known Chinese author Hsu Soo went to hear her at a rally in Hong Kong, and attended it three successive nights to listen to her speak. True, he had heard about her years before, while still in China, when her name had come up in a debate among University students. One of them told of a little foreign woman named Ai Weh Teh who lived in his own town in Shansi, and how she had impressed him with her dedication to the cause of China and her ability to control the children in her charge. Hsu Soo had been interested then, wondering what was the motive power behind this life of sacrifice, so when he had the opportunity to see her it is not surprising that he did so. What is significant is that having heard her, he went again and then again.

Later he wrote about her, likening her to a philosopher

who uses very simple illustrations to make clear a deep and difficult teaching; to a skilful writer, making her main theme significant; to a successful actress who can convey the inward feeling of the person she is representing. Then he went on to write,

"The small women is a very outstanding philosopher, studying topics the past philosophers could never solve. The small woman is also a writer using her life to write a very dramatic history. The small woman is also an actress on the stage of life. God made her one of the greatest figures in our history," and he finished by testifying that from this time on his attitude that Christianity was a figment of the imagination changed. He now believed there was a God in the universe.

Her friends had no cause to fear the effect of what she said when she was just herself, the witty little London parlourmaid recounting her experiences and producing her own evidence that there is a living God. The influence she could exert with her limited ability seemed limitless. It was when she went beyond her ability that she got into difficulties, like a little girl learning to swim who suddenly finds herself out of her depth. Her horror of Communism, born during that nightmare-ish journey across Siberia, fostered by what she knew about the "Red Bandits" in Shansi and what she saw and heard among the refugees in Hong Kong, forced from her statements which were difficult to substantiate when they were challenged. And her generalisations on current affairs sprang from an emotional reaction as much as an informed mind. There were times when the promoters of her meetings had rather anxious little talks with individuals afterwards, trying to explain that Miss Aylward had not meant exactly what she said. . . .

When she left England in 1957, however, she was merely a very well-known missionary whose departure was reported in some religious journals but made little stir elsewhere. *The Small Woman* was released for publication just about the time she left, so although it immediately got good reviews she was not on the spot to be affected by them. She was heading for the Far East, to live again among her people, the Chinese, and that was what interested her.

She arrived in Hong Kong and was almost delirious with excitement as she greeted those who had come to meet her – Chinese and westerners alike, many of whom she had known in China. Hong Kong was the nearest she could ever get to the beloved country, the mainland of China, and it was here that there were the greatest opportunities to help those frightened, destitute refugees from Communism who were still flooding quietly across the well-guarded border. She went among them almost immediately with Michael, a young refugee from Canton, of whom she had heard while still in England, and one of those whom she had been helping to support. She wrote home of the conditions in which the refugees were living, of the poverty.

". . . hundreds of little huts of all shapes and sizes, the only homes these people now know.

"They moved me by their earnestness and keenness, and I wondered how many of you would remain happy under such conditions. Yet every morning at seven the Christians are praying in the little chapel. While I was there, we had torrential rains and many of the huts collapsed and were swept away. Everyone suffered in some way for it is impossible to keep the water out. I gave out the money which had been sent me by the Oxford Committee for Famine Relief."

As her friends knew, that was not all she gave away. The Air Commodore's wife in London received a 'phone call one day from a very irate lady who said she had just returned from Hong Kong where she had visited Miss Gladys Aylward. "I thought you were a friend of hers!" said the very irate lady. "And there she was, living in utter poverty in a little room about eight feet square. . . . I thought you were a friend of hers!"

"So I am," said the Air Commodore's wife. She sighed as she put down the receiver. What was the good of trying to explain to anyone who didn't know Gladys, that however firmly you insisted that *this* money was intended for her and no-one else, you knew as you were saying it that it wouldn't make any difference? And in a place like Hong Kong, among all those refugees, what was the good of expecting that Gladys would spend the money on herself?

But Gladys did not stay in Hong Kong. The decisive act of years ago when she relinquished her British citizenship and became naturalised as a Chinese decided things for her now. In Hong Kong as in England her status was that of an alien, and it is very difficult indeed for an alien to remain permanently in overcrowded Hong Kong. In the autumn of 1957 she went on alone to Formosa, last bastion of the Chinese Nationalists. From that time the little island was her home, the place to which she proudly referred as "Taiwan, Free China."

From Taiwan she sallied forth on her speaking tours

to the U.S.A., Canada, to New Zealand and Australia, to England, to Korea and Japan. In Taiwan she rescued abandoned babies as she had done long ago in Yangcheng, toddled off to preach in mountain villages with Gospel posters under her arm, welcomed lonely youngsters into her home and became their adopted mother. Taiwan was the scene of her greatest joys as well as her deepest sorrows, and in Taiwan her little body lies today.

*     *     *

It was at Taipei, at the extreme north of the island that Gladys settled after the first full and exciting day when she was accorded what amounted to a civic reception, with announcements over the radio that she had arrived. A number of Chinese appeared who claimed to have known her long ago in China, including an elderly gentleman who said he had been in Yangcheng when she was there, and a young woman who insisted that she was a daughter, one of the orphans who she had brought over the mountains. The validity of some of those claims was open to doubt, but of some there could be no question, from officials who had known her in Sian to students she had "mothered" in Chengtu.

Jarvis, stocky and steadfast, was one of these. He was there at the quay to meet her when she arrived. An officer in the Air Force now, he was eager to take her to his home in the south of the island to meet his wife and children. "They are your grandchildren, mother," he told her, and she took them to her heart. Jarvis was always "my eldest son" to her.

She moved around a lot during her first weeks, staying here and there, meeting this one and that one she had known in China. But then she slipped quietly into the sort of life that suited her best. She rented a small room in a Chinese house in a lane on the outskirts of Taipei. And it was when she was walking along that lane, beside which meandered a sluggish stream, that one day she met Esther.

Esther was the wife of an officer in the Nationalist Army. A gentle, smiling, plump little person was Esther, and she loved the Lord Jesus. No-one who met Esther was left long in any doubt about that. There are those who assert that religion is a personal matter and should not be talked about to all and sundry, but Esther did not take that view. Her attitude was that if you had good news the thing to do was to pass it on, and as Gladys was of the same mind the two of them were friends right from the start, when Esther approached her with a smile and said how glad she was to meet her. She had heard about Ai Weh Teh, she said, heard about her heart of love towards God and towards man. Ai Weh Teh must come and visit her, for weren't they both children of God and therefore sisters? And when Esther visited Gladys in return, and quietly observed the privations in which she was living, many were the gifts of food and money she inconspicuously passed on to "her sister".

She did something else, too.

"You are all alone here in Taiwan," she said to one lonely young man who had been brought as a refugee schoolboy to Taiwan when the Communists gained control of the mainland. "Would you like to have a mother here? I know someone who wants a son."

Yes, indeed he would like to have a mother! He was working by day and studying by night, and there was no-

one to call his own, no honourable old one to give him
advice, help him in his difficulties, and pay his respects
to! Indeed he would like to have a mother. So Esther
brought a son to Gladys. Esther didn't stop at one, either.
She was a happy mother of several children herself, and
saw no reason why Gladys should not have a family large
enough to fill her heart which was obviously of consider-
able width. Esther produced several young people, all
eligible in her estimation to join the adopted family of Ai
Weh Teh. An unusual type of match-maker was Esther,
and by no means an unsuccessful one. Over the years
Gladys' animated if not very lucid letters to friends in
England contained endless references to her sons, their
wives and then to her grandchildren, several of whom she
named after members of the Aylward family and her
close friends.

Besides the sons there was Daughter, who claimed
Gladys as "mother" when first she arrived in Taiwan.
Surely Ai Weh Teh remembered her! Ai Weh Teh's
memory might be very bad, but she could not have forgotten! Daughter was married, and Son-in-law soon
became just as dear to Gladys as any of her other "sons".
Gradually it became evident that Daughter and her little
family were closer to Gladys than anyone in Taiwan.

There was only one shadow over her life in those
first years in Taiwan and that was the matter of the filming of her story. The memory of signing that fateful document scarcely crossed her mind until she began receiving
letters asking if she knew what was happening. Did she
realise that a Hollywood film company was making a film
about her? Could she imagine what distortions of her life
would be the outcome? Had she heard who was to im-

personate her? What was she thinking about to allow
this thing to continue? Cheap publicity! Love scenes!
When she was alone in her little room the realisation of
what she had agreed to so naïvely when she put her signature to that contract covered her with a sense of shame,
plunged her in despair, and occasionally stung her into
a fury.

Her letters to her friends sounded desperate. She was
a broken-hearted woman, she told them. When that film
came out none of them would want to have anything
more to do with her, although she did not know what was
in it or what it was all about. She had never had a love
scene as such in her life! It would be best for everybody
to forget all about her. The world could be very nasty, in
fact, it was a very wicked place. She had been besieged
with letters, horrid letters, and if she ever returned to
England, which was very unlikely, they would find her a
very different woman to the one they knew. She would
consider no one, no one at all. And if anyone ever again
put anything into print about her without her permission,
she would sue them immediately. She would not hesitate
a moment.

Everybody, or nearly everybody was against her, she
asserted. The only one who had not failed her was God;
but although she had made many mistakes, especially
letting that film be made, she knew He had forgiven her.
He was wonderful, and she did want to be the best for
Him. The devil had got her down but he hadn't got her
out, and she was going forward, whatever happened,
film or no film. God was with her, and that was all that
mattered. The little girl who "attacked her difficulties
vigorously" when at school in Edmonton lived on in

Gladys. Tear-stained but determined, she continued her pilgrim's progress.

The film was produced under the title of "The Inn of the Sixth Happiness", with many Mikado-like touches, with the tall, beautiful Ingrid Bergman playing the part of Gladys, and with a happy ending of her return into the arms of a tall Eurasian officer in the Chinese Army skilfully implied.

In vain did well-meaning friends try to console Gladys with the assurances that in spite of the obvious distortions it was really a very moving film with quite a high moral tone; and that no intelligent person would pay any attention to the Hollywood-type love scenes, and no-one who knew her would believe they had ever taken place. Gladys refused to be comforted, and she refused to see the film. It was banned from Taiwan, so she never came into direct contact with it. Yet in a remarkable way it brought her into the public eye and opened unexpected doors, largely through her own unconscious action, when she went to America in 1959.

She had decided to re-visit England. This decision was made after some babies had been virtually left on her doorstep. She often told the story of the arrival of one of them.

I was very happy. I was going out preaching every day, as busy as I could be. Then one night, when I got home after a meeting, I found someone had broken in. But they hadn't taken anything.

They'd left something behind. They'd left a baby! There it was lying in my room, and I looked at it and

I said, "Oh no, Lord. No! Definitely no! I don't want any more babies. I'm nearly sixty, and that's too old to have babies ... No, Lord! ..."

Then followed one of her conversations with God which ended with her saying,

"All right, Lord. If you want me to take in babies – all right, Lord!"

So she started taking in babies as well as going out preaching. Daughter and Son-in-law were with her continuously now, and Michael was in Hong Kong working among refugees. There was not enough money for all they wanted to do. Gladys thought of her friends in England, how sympathetic they had been when she told them of the little orphans in Yangcheng, how ready to send clothes to refugees in Hong Kong. Wouldn't they be even more willing to help if she could make them see how the pathetic plight of those little scraps of Chinese humanity that no-one seemed to want, whimpering and crying so weakly in their helplessness?

She would go back to England and tell them about those abandoned babies. She would go by air, though she was a bit scared of aeroplanes, as it would be quicker. She would go to America first.

She did not really know why she felt she should go to America first. She had never been there before, and didn't know anyone, but that made no difference to the feeling that she ought to go that way. It was one of those incomprehensible urges that she got from time to time and, as usual, there was someone on hand to give her the help she never thought of seeking. An American in Taipei cabled to his brother-in-law in the U.S.A. saying a Miss Gladys Aylward would be passing through the country en route for England. She had very little money. Could he help her?

It so happened that his brother-in-law was an executive in World Vision Inc., an organisation that lived up to its name by giving generous help to all sorts of people in all sorts of places. Its President, Dr. Bob Pierce, brought suffering Korea into focus in Christian circles all round the world as he travelled from country to country with a picturesque, winsome, well-trained choir of Korean War orphans dressed in national costume. And Dr. Bob Pierce, so it transpired, had met Gladys Aylward years before, in China. By all means help the little woman! Let her be the guest of World Vision while in the States! A great little person – deserves all the help we can give her!

Gladys was whisked off to Los Angeles, and put up in a hotel at World Vision's expense. At the end of her first week there World Vision Inc. was mystified by the hotel bill. It appeared that Miss Aylward did not eat food. She just occupied a bedroom. No meals had been charged to her account, and later, when they got to know her better, they found out why.

She wasn't used to staying in hotels, she admitted, and didn't realise that all she needed to do was to write a chit for anything she had in the dining room. The price of meals alarmed her, she was afraid she wouldn't have enough money to pay for them, so she crept round to a cheap hamburger stand when no one was about, explained to the waitress that she did not know anything about American food, and would the waitress kindly advise her what to have – not too expensive, please.

World Vision Inc. saw to it that that never happened again!

Shortly after her arrival in Los Angeles she was invited to speak at the Mariner's Club. This was held in the Hollywood First Presbyterian Church, though there is no record that any of the "film giants of Hollywood" were present. About a couple of hundred young people were, though, and they were so impressed by this amazing little woman with her story of faith and courage that they sent a deputation to the minister of the church requesting that she be asked to preach in it. She took the pulpit one Sunday morning, addressing a congregation of over 1,500 people with the same effect as at the Mariner's Club.

Then it got around that this was the very woman whose exploits in China had inspired the writing of the best-selling book *The Small Woman*, and the production of the film, just released, *The Inn of the Sixth Happiness*. She wasn't in the least like the film made her out to be – she was only about five feet high, and her hair was scraped up in two little plaits over the top of her head; she wore a gorgeous Chinese gown but apart from that you wouldn't look at her twice, not until she started to speak. But then – oh boy! You couldn't take your eyes off her then! You could hear a pin drop while she told about the way she went to China because she knew God had called her, and how her senior missionary opened an inn for muleteers and she had to grab the mules – and then the way she whipped round and challenged everybody, were *they* willing to step out for God? Made you feel ashamed of yourself and your flabby faith. . . . You ought to go and hear her. A great little woman. . . .

Gladys did not know when she went there why she had to go, but afterwards she had no doubt that God had launched her into the U.S.A.

CHAPTER FIFTEEN

# *The Falling Star*

The World Vision representative was puzzled. Then he was worried. Something had gone wrong with Gladys and he didn't know what it was. They had been travelling together for weeks, going from one meeting to another all over Canada, and they had got on fine! Indeed, Gladys had told him that she felt he understood her better than any man she knew, which was very gratifying for a young man who had the responsibility of acting as a sort of business manager to a famous missionary speaker nearly twice his age. She confided all sorts of things to him, including the difficulties she had had during her first lonely weeks in the U.S.A., and how angry she had got when people asked her frivolous questions like what food did she eat, had she seen the film, had she met Ingrid Bergman? He had noticed this himself, and had been surprised at the meek way people accepted her retorts. "I think mainly because they realised her depth and because they felt she had suffered and felt deeply about the questions they asked," he explained to someone later.

As far as he and she were concerned, however, they had laughed together and eaten together and prayed together, and never the suspicion of a cloud between them. Then suddenly Gladys had turned morose. He asked her what was wrong. No reply. He couldn't get a word out of her, and sitting opposite to her at meals on trains or in hotels three times a day, plunged in gloomy silence had become quite a strain. He searched his words and his actions to try and find how he might have offended her, but could find nothing.

Eventually, when Sunday came, he could stand it no longer. They were both due to preach at a morning church service, and he knew he would feel like a hypocrite if he did so.

"Gladys," he said. "We've got to have this out. I'm not going to that service until I know what's wrong. I'd be a complete hypocrite, standing up there preaching when there's this undercurrent between us. What have I done to upset you? If you don't tell me so that I can put it right, I refuse to go and preach."

He was utterly unprepared for the answer.

"It's Tibet," she said. Her gloominess had nothing whatever to do with him. She had had an awful premonition, a sort of vision of terrible Communist persecution in Tibet. She hadn't told him because she'd been afraid he would laugh at her, but she had been praying for hours in the night, for Tibet. She couldn't get it out of her mind, what she knew was happening there.

A week later, as they emerged from a restaurant in Toronto, the early noon edition of one of the newspapers was on sale, and the headlines ran "3,000 massacred in Tibet". Gladys saw the announcement, and broke down. If only she had prayed more earnestly, she wept, if only she had entered the spiritual conflict with greater faith and sincerity, those poor people might have been saved! The World Vision representative was silent. Her compassion for suffering humanity that was so evident in her almost reckless involvement of life and possessions was well-known – but this was different. It was not often that Gladys revealed how deeply she plunged into the unseen spiritual realm. Perhaps that was the secret of her unique power to strip off shams and face people with stark reality in her preaching, and of her apparent fearlessness in facing new situations.

"The eagle that soars in the upper air does not worry itself how it is to cross rivers," she wrote once in her Chinese Bible. It took a Gladys Alyward to visit the Chinese offshore island of Kinmen immediately following a terrible bombardment from the Communist guns, get straight down to practical work among the wounded, visit and encourage tiny Christian groups, and so acquit herself as to be officially accorded the title of honorary citizen. Most people would have thought it utterly impossible to obtain permission to visit what was virtually the front line, even if they would not have been deterred by the danger. But Gladys felt God wanted her to go, so she went. Eagles don't worry about how to cross mere rivers!

But eagles encounter storms that the earthbound avoid. When she arrived in Hong Kong after an extensive speaking tour in Australia and New Zealand she was so exhausted that the tour arranged for her in Canada had to be cancelled. Bewildered and battered she made her way up to the Haven of Hope in Junk Bay, where the large-hearted Annie Skau had now opened a sanatorium for T.B. patients. Here she wept and talked and talked and wept. The film. The publicity. The confusion in her mind about those years in China, so far in the past now. The things she had said on the spur of the moment that had been reported. "I wish people wouldn't ask me about those things that happened so long ago. I sometimes wonder if what I tell is truth – or is it imagination?" she sobbed. "I'm scared – scared that I'm not telling the truth. . . ."

"Gladys," said Annie. "You must stay here. Stay here with me. You need rest. We can help you here." So Gladys stayed in the Haven of Hope. And in a letter home she explained.

"I have high blood pressure, low blood count and doctor says I am on the edge of a nervous breakdown and must stop all meetings and anything that worries me. But everything does worry and I get horrible dreams. At times I am not sure whether the people or facts are real or a dream" . . . and then she added, "I only know I am trusting *Him* and *He* will see me through."

Weeks passed before she was ready to return to the whirl of her busy life, but as soon as she could face it she was back again. With some Chinese Christian men she had established a little Mission in Kowloon, with Michael in charge, and when she went along to preach the place was crowded. Ai Weh Teh had a reputation not only as a speaker but as a philanthropist, and there was much poverty in the neighbourhood.

But Taiwan was her country, and she was always glad to get back to Taipei city with its street vendors and open-fronted shops, its streams of bright-faced Chinese youngsters, its maze of alleys lying back from the main streets, and to her own little home. There she would return from her speaking tours abroad, and her visits to country churches and student retreats in the island itself, in through the large, double leaved gates to the little paved courtyard, across to the front door of the single storied house, and into the large entrance hall that served as sitting room as well. There were always piles of letters waiting for Gladys, and as soon as she arrived there would be visitors coming in to see her, her "sons" and their children, Esther – and, of course, Daughter and Son-in-law and their family. They lived nearer to her than any of the others. Daughter and Son-in-law were responsible for the running of the orphanage, for which support came from various sources as a result of Gladys' tours abroad.

In some ways, looking after orphans had been easier in Yangcheng than it was in Taipei. It was simple to have a free for all establishment on your own mission compound in a remote part of Shansi, but in Taipei, with its high standards and its modern way of life, you couldn't do it just like that. There was the problem of whether you could have boys over a certain age living in the same house as girls, and whether the servants would look after babies as well as school children, and what you did with the babies if they wouldn't. There was the business of getting a sponsor for each of the children, someone in America or Australia or England who would undertake to pay so much each month for a certain child; and there was the business of sending that person news about the child from time to time, and snapshots. To say nothing of the confusion when the landlord of the place you were renting wanted the place back, and you had to find somewhere else for the children. And even if, providentially, an organisation of warm-hearted Americans was found which had just the right building, beautifully equipped and empty, into which the children could go, another set of problems presented themselves because it then had to be decided whether the children were still yours, or whether they were now the responsibility of the organisation into whose building they had come, so to speak, to roost. And if they weren't yours any more, you had to explain to all the sponsors that their children were now being provided for by someone else, but there were some new ones being left on doorsteps pretty well every day, who were all being taken in and looked after, and would they like to take them on instead?

All these, and more, were the sort of problems that attended the running of an orphanage in Taipei. And if that wasn't enough, there was the unreasonable attitude of governments and organisations towards money. In Yangcheng, when a money order reached you from Mum, or some friendly missionary sent you a few dollars, you simply went and spent the money on what was needed. And as it was always needed immediately, if not by you, certainly by someone else, it was spent immediately. With governments and organisations, however, if you received money you were supposed to enter it up and pass it on so that it could be entered up somewhere else and passed on, and promptly come back to you with very clearly typed instructions that as the donor gave it for such and such a purpose, for such and such a purpose it must be used, and no other. All in order to satisfy governments, fulfil obligations to donors, ensure that auditors could balance the books and secure the right amount on deeds of covenant. And, of course, there were committees. . . .

It was so much simpler if you obeyed the Scriptural injunction not to let your right hand know what your left hand did! And it was more sensible. It left more time for really important things, like going out preaching. So thought Gladys. And if money was given to her for her work, why not use it without all that silly bother?

Altogether, it is not surprising that World Vision Inc. and Gladys eventually decided to run their affairs separately.

"You will know that I personally have nothing more to do with World Vision. I am sorry because they have been very good to me, and I liked to feel I belonged," Gladys wrote early in 1963 to her World Vision friend of the Canadian tour. If she wasn't part of the organisation any longer, it didn't make any difference to the people in it who were her friends. "I do not yet understand where the misunderstanding began. But I am free, and God knows my heart. He has blessed me and the work, and I praise Him. Open doors on every hand. We only need courage and time to go in them. God has given me souls in nearly every meeting I have taken lately. In the prison at Christmas there was a real move, and we praise God it is still going on."

In her little house as she wrote were three babies, one of her "sons" on a short leave from the Navy, and a missionary who had come for the week-end. But Gladys was used to that sort of thing and scribbled away,

"We have eighty-six children in the orphanage." Daughter and Son-in-law made wonderful parents, she said.

"I am well and very happy. Gordon, my baby who just one year ago was left on my step when he was five days old, was very sick for three whole months. All hope was given up, but I claimed him for God and he was wonderfully healed."

She didn't mention that she had looked after the sickly baby herself right from the start until he was so ill he had to be taken into hospital; that it was she who sat by his little cot, night after night, ready to tend him when he needed it; that when she was presented with the hospital bill she looked at it in dismay, and then asked if she could pay it off monthly, please . . . and that the doctor had called out to her from his office, "That's all right, Miss Aylward. No charge." That was all involved in being a mother, and taking in babies for God!

"What a great and wonderful God we have, how small we feel when we realise how great He is. To know He saved and called us is something that I will never really understand; why He should want a person like me who does so many silly things. But I do love Him and want to do His will.

"We are all very busy getting ready for a Billy Graham Crusade. All churches joining in. We are expecting great things. Prayer meetings all over the place and tracts etc. given out, visiting of all homes with invitations so we are busy."

Then she continued,

"I am also, on top of all this, trying to clear up, for on 28th I fly at invitation of B.B.C. to London. I prayed for an open door to see my loved ones there, and here it is." She did not say what the B.B.C. wanted her to do when she got to London, for she did not know! Letters and cables had been speeding their way to America and Asia, as well as in England, in preparation for the "This is Your

Life" programme in which Miss Gladys Aylward was to appear, but she knew nothing of it.

She boarded the plane on 28th March, 1963, to go to London, and she had the chubby little Gordon with her. Couldn't leave him behind! She took him along to the B.B.C., too, although not until she arrived did she know what it was all about.

The millions of people who viewed that programme saw her just as she was – an excited, uninhibited little woman in a Chinese gown, squealing with delight, bright bead-like eyes nearly popping out of her head, as one after another people were introduced to her who had played a part in her life – Violet, her sister, Laurie, her brother, David Davies her fellow missionary in Shansi, Handley Stockley the doctor who had saved her life in Siam, and others ... and then, crowning joy of all, there was handsome young Son-in-law! She could scarcely believe it! She had left him in Taipei only four days before, and here he was, with her, in London. To everybody's delight, she leapt at him, he swept her up in his arms, and the B.B.C. brought to a triumphant unrehearsed conclusion one of the most successful "This is Your Life" programmes they had ever produced.

A few days later the telephone rang in a basement flat at Marble Arch, and Coolie answered it. Gladys was at the other end of the line, and after a word of greeting announced,

"I'm going to lunch with the Queen of England tomorrow."

The Coolie gasped. "You're going to lunch with the Queen?"

"Yes," replied Gladys. "I couldn't tell you before, as

it all had to be very hush-hush. Don't let anyone else know until it's all over, will you."

"What are you going to wear?"

"Oh, it depends on the weather. I may wear what I had on for 'This is Your Life', or I may wear another nice gown I brought with me. See what the weather's like."

"How will you get there?"

"Oh, that'll be all right. I'll just get a taxi. I need a new handbag, though. I'd better ring off now, and go round to Marks and Spencer's to get one ... Do pray the food will be what I can eat, Coolie. You know, there are some things I just can't take, and it would be awful to make a fuss...."

The Coolie walked away from the telephone feeling rather dazed, and perhaps just slightly uneasy. To hail a taxi and pop round to the Palace didn't seem quite the way it ought to be done.

Pastor Wang didn't think so, either. Gladys told him about the invitation, and he asked the same question as the Coolie – How are you going to get there? and when she told him he said,

"But Gladys, you can't do that! You're representing Free China! You can't just go to Buckingham Palace to lunch with the Queen in a taxi. Leave it to me. I'll see to it for you." So the next day a dignified Pastor Wang arrived in a sumptuous car, chauffeured by its owner, a member of the flourishing Chinese Church in London, and escorted her to Buckingham Palace. She arrived in fine style, and when she emerged, there was the car and the escort waiting for her.

Pastor Wang had decided she might as well make a day of it, and had arranged to take her on to visit the Houses of Parliament. That part of his plan did not work so well. Gladys was so obviously bored after about twenty minutes in the House of Commons that he took her on to the House of Lords, and fifteen minutes of that was more than enough. "You can take me back to Marble Arch and drop me there," she said. She wanted to go and tell the Coolie all about it, and scuttled down the iron stairway to the basement flat called Bethany as fast as she could.

Everything had gone off very well. The food was good but simple, and she hadn't any trouble eating it. There were eight guests, and she was the only woman. They'd been allowed to peep into the room where they were to lunch so they could see where they'd be sitting. She'd been put next to Prince Philip, and he was very nice to talk to, she didn't feel in the least bit awkward. The Queen had shown her the flamingoes in the garden, and said they were very difficult to rear. She seemed very touched to receive the embroidered scroll that was presented to her from the orphans in Taiwan, and called her husband over. "Look at this, Philip," she said. "Isn't it lovely?" She said she would have it made into a fire screen.

Altogether, it had been a lovely experience, and a great honour. Gladys and the Coolie agreed on that. Gladys didn't say anything about going to the Houses of Parliament afterwards. There was really nothing to tell. She had enjoyed going to lunch at Buckingham Palace, and found Royalty very easy to get on with – but as for Her

Majesty's ministers of state she didn't know what they were talking about.

\*     \*     \*

Gladys eventually returned to Taiwan accompanied by one of the Trustees who had been looking after her affairs in England. Gladys was delighted. It was wonderful that someone who been supporting the work all these years could see it personally, and so be much better able to tell people in England about the orphanage. As the Trustee knew quite a lot about book-keeping, that side of things could be explained, too. Son-in-law would help.

The books were opened.

The Trustee looked perplexed.

Then the Trustee looked worried.

Then questions were asked....

Then Son-in-law looked angry.

Something was seriously wrong. Shock followed shock. Then a petition was filed in Taipei in which the Superintendent of the Gladys Aylward Orphanage was sued for embezzlement of funds, and the Trustee returned to England. The one best able to give the necessary evidence was on the spot, and she spoke Chinese – Ai Weh Teh.

# CHAPTER SIXTEEN

# Gladys makes a Come-back

The allegation that Son-in-law had been embezzling funds (over one million Taiwan dollars were missing) was the bitterest blow Gladys had in her life. It cut her far more than the publicity brought about by the film. She would not even believe it at first. There must be some mistake! He would never have done it, never! She knew him, she trusted him utterly. Then, as the evidence was produced, item by item, she urged him to confess. If only he would confess some way out would be found! She wept, she threw her arms round Son-in-law and Daughter, pleading with them to repent and confess – in vain.

The next two or three years were the worst Gladys ever knew, for if ever East met West in collision they met then, in her little body. The Western viewpoint was that one who embezzled money donated for helpless orphans must face the Law! Chinese justice agreed. When the matter became known in Taipei, as of course it did, a Very High Official stepped in, saying that it was a disgrace to the Chinese nation that anyone should cheat a woman so known and respected for her self-sacrifice and good works as Ai Weh Teh. The man accused of doing this thing, therefore, since he had been a sergeant in the armed forces, must be tried as a soldier, not as a civilian. Had Gladys not gone to plead against this decision, which carried the maximum penalty, things would have gone much harder for Son-in-law than they did.

All the same, to bring the affair into the light in this way went against the Chinese grain. It shouldn't have been dealt with like that. It shouldn't have been made public. Face should have been saved, and the case settled out of court. But there was no way out now, and the British woman who had become Chinese had to go on with it.

The case became a scandal. It dragged on for two years, and during this time she was quite ostracised. She was already discredited in the eyes of westerners because of her reaction to the film, and now in the eyes of the Chinese because of the court case. Only a few of those closest to her stood by her, quietly trying to comfort her, but by and large she was avoided. There were times, too, when she was acutely aware of active secret antagonism. On one occasion she was threatened by a man who unsheathed a knife and it was probably the providential appearance of a doctor who knew her well that spared her from assault. For all her fearlessness in plunging into unknown situations she had a natural timidity which those who knew her best had often noticed, and during those years there were times when she dreaded being alone in her little house at night.

Worse than that, something seemed to have happened within her own personality. Westerners and Chinese alike observed it. "From trusting everybody she's changed to trusting nobody," they said. Only to her intimate friends did she write of the struggle she had in those days. She felt as though even her faith in God was failing now.

It showed itself in various ways. "Her stock went very

low," said an American missionary who had known her long ago, in China, and had respected her. "Her stock went very low. It went low in the eyes of the westerners, and it went low in the eyes of the Chinese." He paused for a moment, and then he added rather deliberately,

"But she made a come-back."

\*     \*     \*

The inside story of those years she shared with only her most intimate friends. She was so confused that she did practically no preaching.

"I have not taken any meetings now for nearly a year," she wrote to one, a nurse who was running a rehabilitation home for mental patients in the south of England. "I have not been too busy, but too mixed up in my mind. How can I help anyone when I really need help myself? ... I feel I have not been all I should be to you. I wanted to help so much, but these two years have been so tied up. I long to be free, and be able to get out and do what I know is what God called me for. I have stagnated for two years. . . ."

She was conscious of having very few friends. Esther came from time to time, looking at her anxiously, urging her to eat more, putting food in the refrigerator because she knew Gladys did not bother to do anything about it herself. One or another of her "sons" came, sometimes just at the right moment when there was something to be done that needed a man's strength. But she received very few letters. She who had for years got so many that she could not cope with them all, now had days when not one came.

"This has been a most trying and heart-breaking time,

and I wonder many times how I have come through. I have been going to send to you and tell you I was giving up, but it never really came to that. Every time God sent someone or something to remind me that I was His, and He was going to manage."

She felt she knew why the little lad, Gordon, had come to her. She had looked after many of the babies herself until they were either adopted or ready to go into an orphanage, and how she had missed them when she had to part with them! But this one was her own. "I know why God let me have him, for I do not know what I would have done without him. When things were so bad it was as if he knew, bless him."

At one stage her nurse friend was having difficulties in her own work, and Gladys wrote,

"Now, I know exactly what you are going through, because I am going through the same thing. This has been my most terrific year, and I do not believe I could stand another one like it. It seems as though everything I do is wrong, and only my faith in a Loving and Living God keeps me going, because I get one bang after another. The latest is that we have to get out of the building· we are in, where the orphanage is, and so I am busy going around looking for a house. This is something that tires me very much. It takes time and energy and I get tired so quickly, because I have had a really bad summer. I have been up and down all the time, not only with prickly heat, but with a funny head – something like I used to have, you know – blackouts. Well, I can keep going, but only as I trust the Lord.

"So, dear, I believe that God has called you and me," she continued, "and it is not to walk as other people have walked in a nice, rosy way, but just along the way He walked to Calvary; and one day we will be able to look back and understand why all these things have had to be. I shall pray, when I feel so tired and so head-achy and my back aches, for you as your back aches. I shall pray, when I am razzled with money, about your money and I know that as I look for a building I will think of your building. We are walking hand-in-hand along a road which He asks very few people to walk and, as I say, one day we will know and understand why."

In 1966 she paid her last visit to England. The long drawn out court case was over, with Son-in-law sentenced to a term of imprisonment. Perhaps she was thankful to get away for a while from scenes that had been so painful, and sometimes frightening. Back in England there was the same welcome as before, for she was a favourite with the press and the B.B.C., and had become almost a legendary figure.

"Are you Gladys Aylward?" children would come and ask her when they saw her in the street. It was like encountering Joan of Arc or Mary Slessor to be meeting in person someone they heard about in school!

"Yes, that's me," she would answer cheerfully, "And here's Gordon!" The sturdy, chubby little Chinese toddler, accompanied her everywhere. On one occasion some friends had arranged to meet her at a restaurant in the City, and on approaching the place noticed people pausing, bending down slightly, then passing on with a piece of paper in their hands and a smile on their faces. A Billy Graham campaign was in progress and Gordon was handing out advertising leaflets. "People will take them more readily from a child," said Gladys in explanation as her friends greeted her.

She was just the same as she had always been, it seemed to them. Fame hadn't really made any difference to her. She still wore her simple Chinese clothes and flat slippers, her hair was still scraped back into two little plaits and pinned over her head. The only outward evidence she gave of being "Mum's daughter" was that she came out, not in diamante jewellery or saucy hats, but in orchids! She had been given one to wear very early in her tours abroad, and had been so taken with it that she rarely appeared in public without wearing an orchid after that – though it was usually an artificial one!

"She's just the same old Gladys," her friends and family said. And although she knew that she could draw the crowds as no other missionary could, and was in demand in circles to which others of her ilk would have no entrance, she accepted it all with a matter-of-fact simplicity. She'd got quite used to moving among the nobs by this time and quite enjoyed it, she said – it made a nice change! It was none of her doing, though.

"You know, Helen," she said once, as she sat with the Air Commodore's wife, having a confidential chat. "I wasn't God's first choice for what I've done for China. There was somebody else. I don't know who it was …" She stared straight in front of her, her dark eyes glowing like those of a seer, and Helen waited silently. She had seen Gladys in that mood before. There was something fragile, other-worldly about it, that must not be disturbed if the revelation were to be given.

"I don't know who it was – God's first choice. It must have been a man – a wonderful man. A well-educated man. I don't know what happened. Perhaps he died. Perhaps he wasn't willing ... And God looked down ... and saw Gladys Aylward ..."

Suddenly Gladys' forefinger shot out and pointed downward with dramatic suddenness, and she continued,

"And God said – 'Well – she's *willing*!'"

She packed a tremendous lot into those months in England. The memory that was so inaccurate when it came to facts and figures seemed to hold an incredible number of names of people she loved. The families of her friends were her families, and she knew them all. There were visits to schools, some of which had Aylward Houses in them, and there were numerous meetings to address. She appointed new Trustees of the Charitable Trust. Always there were letters to write – to her "sons" and their families in Taiwan, to Michael in Hong Kong, and to Kathleen.

She wrote frequently to Kathleen in those days. Kathleen Langton-Smith had arrived in Taiwan to join her just about the time when Son-in-law's dishonesty was brought to light, and that arrival was one of the most providential happenings in Gladys' life. Kathleen had been a postmistress in Nottingham for some twenty years when she saw Gladys in 1963 in the "This is Your Life" T.V. programme. Until then she had never a thought of going to the Far East to work among Chinese orphans. Her arrival in Taipei a few months later, having sold up her home and uprooted herself completely from her old life was as daring, in its way, as Gladys' arrival in Yangcheng thirty years previously.

"Have you had any experience with children?" Gladys asked her.

"No," replied Kathleen. She was unmarried, and an only child.

What could she do, then?

"I can do accounts," remarked Kathleen. Twenty years in the Post Office had equipped her for that, anyway.

"If God's brought you for nothing else, it's for that!" exclaimed Gladys. It turned out that Kathleen could do quite a lot of other things, too, including adapting herself to life in a new country among people whose language she did not understand. And if history repeated itself when two strong personalities clashed, it repeated itself also in the loyalty of the younger to the older that lasted right to the end.

"It is cold here in England and I do not like it. When the wind is so keen I find it hard to walk round the corners," Gladys wrote to her, "I have cried several times, for I wanted to run back to you all," and added emphatically "I love you, I trust you, I long for you and miss you terribly."

Early in 1967 Gladys went back. To her disappointment, Michael and his wife decided to go to Canada, but there were Chinese Christian men connected with the Hope Mission in Hong Kong who were prepared to take responsibility, and so that work continued. Back in Taiwan there were occasional crises in connection with the Babies' Home as when new premises had to be found in a hurry, but on the whole those last few years were peaceful ones. Chinese officials did their best to ensure that. They knew that Ai Weh Teh had no head for business, so they didn't bother her with it. Legalities required of others were by-passed in her case. If you know your man, you can trust him says the wisdom of the ancient East, and they knew her.

And Gladys made her come-back.

She made no effort to do so, of course. It would not have occurred to her to try and make herself popular. She just went on doing the same things in the same way. If there were arrangements to be made in connection with her work, she made them herself, without trying to get help from anyone else. She was quite astute in some ways, and dealt with a Chinese businessman who would not return money he owed her, in a good old-fashioned Chinese way. When he held a large reception she gate-crashed quietly, sat down among the guests and aired her grievance to them. Consternation! The host could not refute what she said, and did not try to do so. Self-appointed middlemen scurried to and fro, but Gladys, tearful yet composed, refused to be silenced. For centuries wives (or daughters-in-law) who could stand things no longer had obtained alleviation of their lot by appealing to public opinion in an outcry in the street, and the method still worked. The affair was settled promptly, out of court, and Gladys got her money back! But those in need knew that the compassionate Ai Weh Teh was the one to go to. She was there like a flash if someone was in distress. Unwanted babies gravitated mysteriously in her direction. The longing to spend all her time at the Babies' Home was strong, for from the time when, as a little girl, she scampered home from school day after day to wheel Laurie out in his pram and help give him his bath, she had loved babies. When requests came to her to speak at meetings here and there, all over Taiwan, she sometimes went grudgingly – but she went.

"Lord, keep me strong in the sense of Thy call," she had written in her Bible years before, and she knew what that call was. She had to tell people about God – her God, the Living God. She hated Communism. Didn't Communism deny the existence of God? Therefore she, Ai Weh Teh, hated it, and didn't hesitate to say so when occasion demanded it. There was no staying neutral on that point, where she was concerned. But her main theme, as always, was the exploits of that silly little Gladys Aylward, and the greatness of her God.

As 1969, the last year of her life dawned, this was what she spoke about at the New Year's meeting she had been asked to address at the U.S. Base in Taipei. She was a frequent visitor there, for although the "Inn of the Sixth Happiness" had been banned in Taiwan, it had had a good run in the U.S.A., and many of the Americans who were stationed in Taiwan had seen it. The tiny heroine was in great demand among them, up and down the island. So at the beginning of 1969 she spoke to some of them and harked back, as she had done so many times before, to that fateful day when she boarded the train to start on her long journey to China.

... And I looked at that little group of people on the platform. They were there to say goodbye to me. They were my friends. And as the train started to move, I said to myself, "Well, that's the last I shall see of them." And I wanted to cry.

But I didn't cry, because suddenly some words flashed into my mind. "Give Me two, and I'll give you five. Give Me five and I'll give you twenty...." something I'd read in the Bible.

Gladys gave a little giggle. "I didn't remember it right," she admitted. Then she added firmly, "But I remembered it the way I believe God wanted me to!" And she continued,

Twentyfold – Sixtyfold – Hundredfold! And I said, "Lord I'm giving up my mother and my father – I want mothers and fathers wherever I go! There's my sister and my brother – Lord, I want sisters and brothers wherever I go! I'm giving you my friends, Lord, that little group of people there on the platform. Lord, I want friends wherever I go...."

And she received them, all the way along the line – one hundredfold.

The last year of her life slipped by. It was a happy year. She had a car, provided through legacies, and although she could not drive, Kathleen could, and this eased things a lot for her. Two or three times a week she was driven the seven miles to the Babies' Home, and spent hours playing with the toddlers there. Gordon who lived with her was a little schoolboy now, and far too big for babies, but Saturday afternoons were often spent by the sea, splashing about with him in a secluded cove. He frequently went with her to the meetings she addressed, and although he was no better than any other little boy in private life, he behaved remarkably well on the platform, smiling rather solemnly when she referred to him as the bundle of rubbish she had picked up, a baby just five days old. But beforehand he often said warningly "Don't talk too long, Mummy!"

One night in the autumn there was a typhoon which struck Taipei with such violence that roofs were ripped off, trees crashed, and rain poured down surging through the narrow alleys, gurgling under gateways and doors, right into the houses. Water poured down from the flat roof of the Babies' Home and the stairways became like waterfalls. Kathleen phoned in desperation to the U.S. Army chaplain who lived nearby, and he went along immediately, dodging sheets of corrugated iron that hurtled along the street like skilfully thrown discs, and after some hours managed to stem the flood. The little house in the city did not escape either, and Gladys reported afterwards that as the water came rushing in Gordon with gleeful excitement suggested that they should pray to God to send a submarine.

Just about this time Gladys started preparing for Christmas, by buying hundreds of dainty calendars with Chinese pictures to send to her friends. She hadn't always been able to do it but this time she wrote little letters as well to personal friends, to donors, to fellow missionaries, to schools she had visited in England.

Her thoughts went back to years of long ago. London. She had two illustrated tea cloths of London scenes stuck up in a corner of her drab little bedroom – St. Paul's Cathedral, a policeman on duty, a red pillar box and a newsvendor huddled with his coat collar up displaying a poster "Evening Special! Summer late this year." How lovely it would be if Violet could be with her! It would be like old times to have her own sister again. "Violet is being very good to us right now. She's been wonderful since Bill died," she wrote to Coolie. "I wish she would come out here, and spend a bit of time. I'd love it."

But if her own blood relations were on the other side of the world, those who were hers by adoption were very near at hand, and the house was astir because of them. Presents for everyone, right down to the latest grand-child! Gladys could not help giving presents. She was addicted to it.

1970 dawned. The weather was damp and chilly, and there were a lot of colds about. Gladys had one, and it made her feel rotten.

"You ought to stay in bed," said Kathleen. "You're not fit to go out."

"Must go out," said Gladys firmly. "Got to speak at that New Year meeting to women at the U.S. Base."

"Ought not to go," mumbled Kathleen but she knew it would be useless to try and prevent her. "If you insist on going I won't go to the Babies' Home today. I'll take you to the meeting by car and bring you back, and see you safely tucked up in bed."

Gladys went to the meeting, preached for over an hour, as usual, and returned very tired. Yes, she'd go to bed. She felt rotten.

Kathleen phoned the doctor. He came about six p.m., said the patient had flu and a touch of pleurisy, gave her an injection. She settled down for a while after that. Gordon got into his little bed on the opposite side of the room and went fast asleep. Kathleen crept out, but she couldn't really rest. She went in and out of the room every hour or two. Gladys had thrown her blankets off – Kathleen replaced them. Gladys was very quiet. Gladys hadn't moved. Then Kathleen touched her hand and it was very cold.

Kathleen caught her breath and stood very still. Then she went quietly over to the other bed, picked up the sleeping boy, head nodding over her shoulder and backed out of the room.

\*     \*     \*

The little body was left alone, dark eyes staring up at the ceiling, the two illustrated tea cloths of London on the wall.

But of course Gladys was not there. When the news flashed round the world, and her death was announced over the B.B.C. she was not there, nor when long crowds of silent Chinese filed past the glass-topped coffin at the lying-in-state either. The funeral service in Taipei was attended by more than a thousand people, and memorial services were held for her in all sorts of places in America, Australia, England, but it all meant nothing to her. It could not affect her, not even when they buried the little body in the soft earth on a hill that faced towards the mainland of China, towards the city of Yangcheng, where they knew her heart had been all these years.

It was all in the past, and she was not there any more. She had moved on to join those who, like her, had given evidence that they knew they were only on pilgrimage, seeking a city of more lasting substance than any they could find in Time. It did not even matter that, as with the patriarch so with the parlourmaid, the promise had been fulfilled "I will make thy name great." The only thing that mattered now was that on rendering her account to her Maker she could do it without shame. For, as she wrote once to a diffident teenager:

"Don't worry about your education.

"God won't ask you for certificates; He'll only ask if you've been faithful to your call."